Dreamers and Stargazers

*Creative Liturgies for
Incarnational Worship:
Advent to Candlemas*

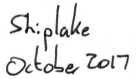
Chris Thorpe

CANTERBURY
PRESS
Norwich

© Chris Thorpe 2017

First published in 2017 by the Canterbury Press Norwich
Editorial office
3rd Floor, Invicta House
108–114 Golden Lane
London EC1Y 0TG, UK

www.canterburypress.co.uk

Canterbury Press is an imprint of Hymns Ancient & Modern Ltd
(a registered charity)

Hymns Ancient & Modern® is a registered trademark of
Hymns Ancient & Modern Ltd
13A Hellesdon Park Road, Norwich,
Norfolk NR6 5DR, UK

'To a Grandchild', p. 100, is from *A Christmas Sequence and other
Poems*, The Amate Press, 1989, and used by permission of the
Estate of the late John V. Taylor.

Scripture quotations are from the New Revised Standard Version of the
Bible, Anglicized Edition, copyright © 1989, 1995 by the Division of
Christian Education of the National Council of the Churches of Christ in
the USA. Used by permission. All rights reserved.

British Library Cataloguing in Publication data

A catalogue record for this book is available
from the British Library

978 1 84825 971 3

Typeset by Regent Typesetting
Printed in the UK by CPI Group Ltd

Contents

Dedicated to
Sarah, Sophie and Jake,
to Rachel and Theo

Introduction
What is Incarnational Worship?

Much of our worship in churches has been designed for people who are familiar with the traditions and content of the Christian faith; but today, many people who do not share that familiarity can find our worship distancing and difficult to connect with. If we turn in on ourselves, and turn our back to the world around us, we are in danger of becoming self-serving.

So these acts of worship start from a different place. They start with our experience of human life, using language that does not rely on religious familiarity and formulation. This worship grows out of the joys and sorrows of our lives in relationship, as communities, and in the wider world. It leads to an opportunity to offer ourselves, engaging wholeheartedly with the process of becoming the good news we proclaim.

The incarnation is a paradox, a mystery – God becoming one of us in the life of Jesus Christ, connecting heaven and earth. These acts of worship are incarnational: they speak of the divine, but from a perspective that is earthed, rooted and grounded in human lived experience. They are incarnational too because they invite us to be fully involved, participating and creating the worship, opening ourselves to allow the word to become flesh in us. Incarnational worship resists the false separation of secular and spiritual, and recognizes that we are whole people: body, mind and spirit. Worship has often engaged our minds, but incarnational worship seeks to involve our heart and gut as well!

Essentially, these resources are an invitation to experience silence, in a shared contemplative space. It is easy for our worship to pile words upon words, barely drawing breath in our talking at God! The real transformative encounter comes when we stop talking and allow space for reflection and listening both to our own inner voice and to the still, small voice of God. There is so little silence in our noise-packed, information-crowded, activity-paced lives; so these moments can be an oasis of calm in a frenetic world, and can allow us to discern what is really going on in our lives, connecting us with ourselves and with God.

Creative prayer for incarnational worship is centred on an encounter with the living God that can change our perceptions and our actions. Each act of worship is intended to open up the possibility of change in us, for us to be different as a result of our encounter with God. This is not worship for its own sake, or as religious entertainment, but worship that expands our horizons, as we connect with the living God and with our topsy-turvy world, in all its pain and possibility. It can be transformational, if we risk opening our hearts and lives to be changed by it.

Advent is an invitation to a radical shake-up in our thinking and feeling. Its themes of impending disaster, judgement and a need to change connect us to the global challenges we are facing in climate change, poverty, inequality, intolerance and migration. Where December has become so overburdened with commercial and social pressures, we can too easily lose the sense of expectation – the hoping and waiting that are at the heart of Advent. Yet our worship can offer a very real alternative to the mad headlong rush, and allow people to ground themselves, to maintain their balance, through December. We can create sanctuary, stillness, silence and a point of perspective that the world cannot give.

Christmas can overwhelm us with its massive expectations of a 'perfect' celebration. It is so puffed up, and so suddenly gone, that we can feel disoriented and disappointed. At the heart of our worship at Christmas are two themes. In Jesus, God comes 'down to earth', and shows us the human face of divine love in the midst of the mess and the muddle of life. In Jesus 'we are all included' in the loving purposes of God, paradoxically particularly when we feel distant. There is an important reconnection needed: the good news of Christ's birth is good news for the whole of our lives, including the darker side that the tinsel of Christmas often obscures. We need the gritty reality of a faith that is not afraid of this darkness. New Year gives us the opportunity to look back on the past, and carry forward the learning that comes with deep reflection.

Epiphany brings a huge canvas for our engagement with the world around us, focusing on moments when people have seen with great clarity who Jesus is, and what he can mean for us. So who is Jesus in a global, multifaith world? How do we live with difference – differences of faith and differences of culture? Why was Jesus baptized? Why are we so driven in our lives? How can we deal with our insecurity? How can we be a blessing for our community? Finally, Candlemas, when Mary and Joseph brought the child Jesus to the Temple, explores themes of light and darkness, of sacrifice, opposition and freedom.

These acts of worship may be used by individuals, small groups or in larger settings as frameworks for silence and reflection. They have been used in church services, in quiet days, retreats, and at the end of small group discussions.

Planning and preparation

It is helpful to invite people to participate in preparing and in leading worship. It can be good to invite a group of people to come together to plan and to prepare for the service. A range of voices and faces leading worship can encourage people to identify more readily with the liturgy.

Context

The liturgies are intended to help people to reflect deeply on their personal faith, so time given to arranging an intimate setting will be well spent. Seating, lighting, the shape and ambience of the room will all be important. Attention to posture and stillness will allow people to enter into the worship more fully. Even large church buildings can be made to feel more intimate with the careful use of lighting.

Visual focus

To worship God as whole people, as body, mind and spirit, it can be helpful to have a visual focus, to create 'stations' in different places, or to gradually build up a place of encounter. Leaders can involve other members of the team in creating a strong visual focus, using a wide range of materials, and objects from the natural world, projected images, art and colour.

Creating a service sheet/PowerPoint presentation

The liturgies in this book are set out for the worship leader, with full notes for running the service, reflections and often the full Bible passage. This is not the format that would be used for a service sheet or PowerPoint presentation. Here you would just want to show a running order, with words of prayers and chants, details of hymns/songs and readings, and other general instructions. At the end of the book are two sample service sheets that give an idea how these might be set out.

Pace

The liturgy is intended to be spacious, taken slowly and with pauses to allow people to reflect deeply on their experience. It is good to hear a variety of voices, so it may be possible to invite people to participate in reading different sections.

Silence

Silence is the key to the whole liturgy, but the leader may need to gauge how much silence a particular group can cope with. If people are completely unused to silence, it may feel uncomfortable at first. It is essential to introduce the silence, and say how long the silence will last, so that people know what is going to happen. Some people may need a question to take with them into the silence, something to think about; others may be comfortable with a word of Scripture, such as, 'Be still and know that I am God', or the Jesus prayer, 'Lord Jesus Christ, Son of God, have mercy on me', or perhaps a phrase related to the theme. As the leader it is important that you are not afraid of the silence, and that you don't 'panic' into ending it early!

Responses

The responses are in bold type, and there are opportunities where these may be said or sung, or replaced with a chant or chorus from Taizé or Iona or elsewhere.

Music

The use of music in the times of reflection is intended to offer yet another 'way in' to the silence. Music speaks to another part of our selves. We have found that less familiar music can add to the creative experience for people, taking them into unfamiliar places! Pieces by James MacMillan, Karl Jenkins, Arvo Pärt, Erkki-Sven Tüür, John Tavener and Gyorgy Ligeti, as well as more ancient music by Byrd, Palestrina, Hildegard of Bingen and Tallis, have all been effective. Music from Taizé and Iona can give a reflective feel too. Just one thing to watch for: be aware that music with words can sometimes be a diversion, with the words getting in the way for some people.

Endings

It is important to have a proper ending for a service. The final prayer will often be the signal for this, and will give permission for people to leave. In some settings, it can be good to play further music after the liturgy, and allow people time to continue to be still while others leave quietly.

ADVENT

Waiting and Hoping

New words for the lighting of the Advent candles

Introduction

Many churches will choose to light a candle for each week of Advent, to remember those who prepared the way for Jesus to come. These words are intended to be used to accompany the lighting of the candles on the Advent ring. They may be used at the very start of the service, or around the Gospel reading, or just before the address. You might like to choose a person to lead each week who represents each of these themes in their life or ministry: for example, a child for hope, an older person for promise, a teenager for challenge, someone exploring ministry for calling, a mother and child for life.

ADVENT SUNDAY

Light of hope

O come, O come, Emmanuel.
Come, Lord Jesus.

The first candle is lit

We dare to light a light of hope,
despite the darkness of our world.
In the face of cruelty and suffering,
of oppression and inequality,
we dare to hope!

In a world that sometimes seems hopeless,
we dare to hope!
With the patriarchs of old,
we dare to hope!
We light a candle in the darkness,
we dare to hope!

O come, O come, Emmanuel.
Come, Lord Jesus.

ADVENT 2

Light of promise

O come, O come, Emmanuel.
Come, Lord Jesus.

The second candle is lit

We come to light a light of promise,
to remember we are not alone,
not abandoned, not lost,
but held in the promise of God's love.

In a world that sometimes forgets God-with-us,
we cling to your promise.
With the prophets of every age,
we cling to your promise.
We light a candle in the darkness,
we cling to your promise.

O come, O come, Emmanuel.
Come, Lord Jesus.

ADVENT 3

Light of challenge

O come, O come, Emmanuel.
Come, Lord Jesus.

The third candle is lit

We receive the light of challenge,
acknowledging much that needs to change,
in our lives,
in our attitudes,
our choices,
and in our world.

In a world of comfort and plenty,
where many go hungry,
challenge us to change.
With John the Baptist,
and all the uncomfortable voices,
challenge us to change.
We light a candle in the darkness,
challenge us to change.

O come, O come, Emmanuel.
Come, Lord Jesus.

ADVENT 4

Light of calling

O come, O come, Emmanuel.
Come, Lord Jesus.

The fourth candle is lit

We affirm the calling of God,
and light a light to say 'Yes'
to that vocation in our lives.
When life seems empty or meaningless,
we embrace that gift of calling.

In a world of conflicting ambitions and drives,
let it be with me according to your word.
With Mary may we say,
let it be with me according to your word.
We light a candle in the darkness,
let it be with me according to your word.

O come, O come, Emmanuel.
Come, Lord Jesus.

CHRISTMAS DAY
Light of life

Emmanuel, God is with us!
Born as one of us.

The central candle is lit

We light a light to celebrate life,
the life of a tiny child,
born in obscurity and danger,
the promise of God with us,
in every part of our lives.

In a world that sometimes seems hopeless,
we dare to hope!
In a world that sometimes forgets God-with-us,
we cling to your promise!
In a world of comfort and plenty,
where others go hungry,
challenge us to change!
In a world of many ambitions and drives,
let it be with me according to your word!

Emmanuel, God is with us!
Born as one of us!

Let There Be Greening

The greening of the church and our lives

Introduction

To prepare for this service it will be good to identify where in church you will be able to hang the greenery. You may need to provide some hooks or other temporary fixings. The green boughs could be large or small depending on the impact you want to make and the space you have available. One great way of involving people and raising the anticipation is to ask different people to bring in the various branches, and to carry them up in the service to decorate the church. You will need branches of cedar, holly and ivy, a Christmas tree and a sprig of mistletoe. Another way of involving everyone is to have lots of small sprigs of each 'green' in a basket, and to invite people to take a sprig and to place it on a windowsill or ledge as part of the service, or as the service concludes.

ADVENT SUNDAY

Prelude – *music is played/sung*

O viriditas digiti Dei – Hildegard of Bingen

The glory of Lebanon shall come unto you, the cypress, the plane and the pine, to beautify the place of your sanctuary. *Isaiah 60.13*

Hymn/Song/Chant – *suggestions*

Touch the earth lightly

I, the Lord of sea and sky

Blessed be your name

Wait for the Lord (Taizé)

Welcome and Introduction

Advent is a time to renew our energy, to gather our strength, to take a fresh look at the way we live our lives as disciples of Jesus. We come to listen to the heart of God, to be open to the abundance of God's grace for us, as individuals, as a church, as communities and as part of the whole of creation. Abbess Hildegard of Bingen in the twelfth century spoke about the 'greening of God', which she called 'viriditas', the creative energy of God, holding all creation in being. Today we need to hear again the impact of her words. We consume so much, but we are empty. Our way of life is damaging our planet; we need to change our ways. In this Advent greening, we will deck the church with symbols of 'viriditas', the creative energy of God, and through them explore what is needed for us, all people and all creation to flourish and know the abundance of God's grace.

Opening Prayer

Greening God,
life of every life,
energy of creation,
be with us now.
Flow in our hearts, generously;
work in our lives, deeply;
help us to change our ways, sustainably;
that we may follow in the footsteps of your Son, Jesus.
Amen.

GREENING OUR WORLD
The cedar

The trees of the Lord are watered abundantly, the cedars of
Lebanon that he planted.
Psalm 104.16

Cedar is a close-grained hardwood, full of resin. Cedar trees are
strong, tall and majestic. They were used in the construction of
Solomon's Temple in Jerusalem. The resinous wood was also used
for ritual cleansing, and for preserving. So we bring in a bough of
cedar to represent the greening of God, the energy of creation that
Hildegard called 'viriditas'.

The cedar is brought into church

Reading

The Word is living, being, spirit, all verdant greening,
   all creativity.
This Word manifests itself in every creature.
Fire of the Holy Spirit, life of the life of every creature,
holy are you in giving life to forms.
Rivers spring forth from the waters, earth wears her
   green vigour.
(Hildegard of Bingen)

Hildegard contrasted this greening power of God with its opposite, 'ariditas' or dryness: 'Now, in the people who were meant to
be green there is no more life of any kind. There is only shrivelled
barrenness.'

Reflection

Often we think of our walk with God, our discipleship with Jesus, as a personal task: about our private life, about spirituality and faith. But Hildegard expands our horizons, pointing us back to God in the whole of creation. We are only a small part of the immensity of this world, and we are not separate, but completely dependent on the whole. So today we start with the cosmos, the big picture of God's generous, overflowing provision. We acknowledge the impact of global climate change and our destructive part in it. We look at the way human beings have acted like asset-strippers, taking resources without thought for the future, wasting and polluting the earth, without care for the real impact and cost. Now, before it is too late and all is turned to 'shrivelled barrenness', we ask how we can change, to live more sustainably.

Reading – *Genesis 1.29–31*

God said, 'See, I have given you every plant yielding seed that is upon the face of all the earth, and every tree with seed in its fruit; you shall have them for food. And to every beast of the earth, and to every bird of the air, and to everything that creeps on the earth, everything that has the breath of life, I have given every green plant for food.' And it was so. God saw everything that he had made, and indeed, it was very good. And there was evening and there was morning, the sixth day.

Response

Living Word of God,
speak within our hearts.

Music for Reflection – *suggestion*

O viriditas digiti Dei – Hildegard of Bingen

How do we personally, and collectively, need to change our ways to protect our planet?

Prayers of Recognition

Greening God, source of all life,
all goodness, all creativity,
we thank you,
for all that is growing and fruitful in our lives,
for all that is abundant and overflowing,
for the energy of creation,
for the delicate balance of the natural world,
and for the diversity and beauty of our environment.
We thank you, O loving God.

Greening God, we are sorry,
where we have consumed the resources of our world without
    care or thought,
where we have damaged and polluted our environment,
where we have disturbed the balance of nature, changing
    our climate.

We are sorry, O loving God.
Forgive our heedless consumption,
forgive our careless pollution,
forgive our selfish accumulation.
Forgive us and help us to change.
Holy Spirit, breathe your healing grace
into our shrivelled barrenness,
fill us with your abundant greening life,
make us as strong as the cedar,
so that we become living temples of your love,
rooted and grounded, with Jesus our cornerstone.
Amen.

Greening God,
you see through our shrivelled barrenness,
to the wellspring of your life,
deep within us.
May your living water flow in us,
transforming our lives,
to dwell in your generous grace.
Amen.

Hymn/Song/Chant – *suggestions*

The cedar of Lebanon, plant of renown

O come, O come, Emmanuel

Great is the darkness

Kyrie (Taizé)

GREENING OUR COMMUNITY
The holly and the ivy

The evergreen leaves of the holly and the ivy have long been popular as Christmas decorations, as symbols of the eternal, unchanging love of God, and the promise of resurrection life. Ivy usually grows up some form of physical support: it has to rely on another tree to grow. We need to recognize that we rely on one another and on God for our support. The holly has been rich in symbolic meaning, representing various Bible scenes – Moses' burning bush from the Old Testament, and from the New Testament both the Virgin Mary and the crown of thorns. In Scandinavia, the holly is known as the Christ Thorn, with its red berries reminding us of the drops of blood shed by Jesus. The holly reminds us that the rich heritage of our faith is woven into the natural world. Today we bring in the holly and the ivy to help us to focus on the greening of our community.

The holly and the ivy are brought into church

Reflection

As Christians we haven't always been good at acknowledging that we need to rely on other people; like the ivy, we need support. We have often worked independently as individuals or as churches, preferring to adopt the culture of self-reliance. Our society values self-made men and women, and looks down on those who acknowledge their need for support. One of the key questions a church needs to ask is, 'Where is God working in our community?' To find the answer, simply look for where the greening energy, the viriditas, is to be found. Often it is outside the church: perhaps in the local school or in a community group. Our task is to go and join in with that energy, rather than to work independently – and that may demand proper humility of the church. The ivy reminds us of the interdependence of all elements of our wider community, where the church needs to acknowledge and work with God's viriditas wherever it is found in the community. As this next reading reminds us, the leaves of the tree of life are for the health of the whole community, for the 'healing of the nations'.

Reading – *Revelation 22.1–7*

Then the angel showed me the river of the water of life, bright as crystal, flowing from the throne of God and of the Lamb through the middle of the street of the city. On either side of the river is the tree of life with its 12 kinds of fruit, producing its fruit each month; and the leaves of the tree are for the healing of the nations. Nothing accursed will be found there any more. But the throne of God and of the Lamb will be in it, and his servants will worship him; they will see his face, and his name will be on their foreheads. And there will be no more night; they need no light of lamp or sun, for the Lord God will be their light, and they will reign for ever and ever.

And he said to me, 'These words are trustworthy and true, for the Lord, the God of the spirits of the prophets, has sent his angel to show his servants what must soon take place.'

'See, I am coming soon! Blessed is the one who keeps the words of the prophecy of this book.'

Response

Living Word of God,
speak within our hearts.

Music for Reflection – *suggestion*

O nobilissima viriditas – Hildegard of Bingen

Where is God at work in our community? Where is the energy?
How can we join in and support this work?

Intercession

Response

Their leaves will not wither.
Their leaves are for healing.

Gracious God,
we pray for the natural world around us in all its diversity.
We thank you for your abundant goodness in creation
and pray that we can learn to nurture and protect
the good gifts you have given us.
Give us the will to adapt and change our ways,
to honour your gift of greening.
We pray for your ever-green love,
to flow freely in the natural world again.

Their leaves will not wither.
Their leaves are for healing.

Gracious God, we pray for our local community,
the places where we live, work and belong.
We bring to you all that is good,
the sharing of trust, of vision and energy for change.
We bring to you all that is dried up, shrivelled and barren,
our local disappointments, frustrations and failures.
We pray for your ever-green love to flow freely in our
    communities again.

Their leaves will not wither.
Their leaves are for healing.

Gracious God, we pray for our family, and church family,
where we hope to be held and loved, cherished and supported.
We thank you for the gift of loving relationships,
of growing trust and mutual care.
We bring to you those relationships we find difficult,
families and churches where love has been fractured and divided,
We pray for your ever-green love to flow freely in our families
and churches again.

Their leaves will not wither.
Their leaves are for healing.

Gracious God, we pray for one another, our deepest needs.
We thank you for the gift of life in all its fullness,
for energy, joy, delight and vitality.
We pray for all whose lives are more of a struggle,
through illness, disability, loneliness or grief.
We pray for the ever-green love of God to flow freely in
us again.

Their leaves will not wither.
Their leaves are for healing.

Gracious God,
we hold all these prayers
in the flow of your greening love,
and in the name of your living word,
Jesus Christ our Lord.
Amen.

Hymn/Song/Chant – *suggestions*

For the healing of the nations

Break our hearts, with the things that break yours

Nothing can trouble (Taizé)

GREENING OUR FAMILY AND OUR CHURCH FAMILY

The Christmas tree

They are like trees planted by streams of water, which yield their fruit in its season, and their leaves do not wither. In all that they do, they prosper.
Psalm 1.3

The Christmas tree holds together so many traditions. In early times, in the medieval paradise plays, fir trees were decorated with fruits to represent the tree of life from the Garden of Eden. Martin Luther introduced Christmas tree candles, to recreate the starlit sky of the first nativity. When all appears dead and bare in the winter cold, the Christmas tree in its vibrant greenness can be a symbol of the promise of eternal life and the gift of new life in the birth of baby Jesus. So the Christmas tree can represent for us the promise and fruitfulness that Jesus can bring to our lives.

However, in some churches, the Christmas tree is later stripped and set aside, and cut to form a rough cross for Good Friday. So the Christmas tree also foreshadows Jesus' crucifixion, nailed to a tree. When Christ the carpenter is killed on a cross of wood, this is the ultimate misuse of the goodness of God's greening creation.

At this time, we come together as families at home and as the family of God here in church to decorate our Christmas trees, gathering together to celebrate an evergreen life that goes deeper than all the challenges of church and family life.

Today we bless the green Christmas tree in church. We acknowledge the times when our family life and the life of the family of the church has failed to honour the goodness of God's greening, and come back to the deep, evergreen goodness of the love that is at the heart of our families and our church family.

Blessing the Christmas tree

You may choose to use this blessing for your Christmas tree at home too

Greening God,
life of every life,
energy of creation.
Bless to us the tree of life,
hold us in our loving.
Bless to us the hidden cross,
hold us in our hurting.
Bless to us the gathering together,
hold us in our connection.
Through Jesus the one who is to come.
Amen.

Reading – *Psalm 96.11–13*

Let the heavens be glad, and let the earth rejoice;
let the sea roar, and all that fills it;
let the field exult, and everything in it.
Then shall all the trees of the forest sing for joy
before the Lord; for he is coming,
for he is coming to judge the earth.
He will judge the world with righteousness,
and the peoples with his truth.

Response

Living Word of God,
speak within our hearts.

Reflection

Do we feel that our families and our church family are alive with the 'viriditas' of God, or struggling through a time of shrivelled barrenness? We can probably sense both at different times.

Where in our family and our church family do we feel flat and exhausted, dry and fruitless? Is it time to prune and to lay down some of these things?

Where is the energy in our family and our church family? Where are the green shoots of life? In this coming year, how can we nurture these growing points?

Music for Reflection – *suggestion*

Jesus Christ the apple tree

Prayer

O Christ, the master carpenter,
who at the last, through wood and nails,
purchased our whole salvation,
wield well your tools in the workshop of your world,
so that we who come rough-hewn to your bench
may here be fashioned to a truer beauty by your hand.
We ask it for your own name's sake.
Amen.
(Traditional)

Hymn – *suggestion*

O Christmas tree

GREENING IN ME

The mistletoe

Peace I leave with you; my peace I give to you. I do not give to you as the world gives. Do not let your hearts be troubled, and do not let them be afraid.
John 14.27

Reflection

Kissing under the mistletoe is a recent addition to the Christmas celebrations! Centuries ago, Norsemen saw the mistletoe as a symbol of peace and hope. Some stories tell of enemies in Roman times meeting under the sanctuary of the mistletoe, laying down their weapons and declaring a truce with a kiss of peace. As we bring in the mistletoe to complete our hanging of the Advent greens, we think about our own sense of peace in our lives – the sometimes precarious balance between our own weariness and our own energies for this coming year. We ask for God's greening in our lives.

The mistletoe is brought into church

Reading – *Romans 12.9–21*

Let love be genuine; hate what is evil, hold fast to what is good; love one another with mutual affection; outdo one another in showing honour. Do not lag in zeal, be ardent in spirit, serve the Lord. Rejoice in hope, be patient in suffering, persevere in prayer. Contribute to the needs of the saints; extend hospitality to strangers.

Bless those who persecute you; bless and do not curse them. Rejoice with those who rejoice, weep with those who weep. Live in harmony with one another; do not be haughty, but associate with the lowly; do not claim to be wiser than you are. Do not repay anyone evil for evil, but take thought for what is noble in the sight of all. If it is possible, so far as it depends on you, live peaceably with all. Beloved, never avenge yourselves, but leave room for the wrath of God; for it is written, 'Vengeance is mine, I will repay, says the Lord.' No, 'if your enemies are hungry, feed them; if they are thirsty, give them something to drink; for by doing this you will heap burning coals on their heads.' Do not be overcome by evil, but overcome evil with good.

Response

Living Word of God,
speak within our hearts.

Reflection

How much of our energy is dissipated in damaged relationships? To be in conflict, to harbour resentments, to hold a grudge, all are exhausting. God longs for us to live in harmony, in genuine love, in peace; but we can find it so hard. Can this Advent be a time of making peace, of being reconciled?

Our making of peace comes on different levels. It may be personal, making peace with ourselves. It may be with another person who has hurt you, moving forward in a relationship where there is discord. It may be spiritual, making peace with God when you have been angry or disappointed. It may be corporate, needing to be reconciled as a community or a nation.

Who do you need to make peace with?

What is blocking the way to peace, preventing you from living in harmony?

What do you need to share with God to be at peace?

Music for Reflection – *suggestion*

O viridissima Virga ave – Hildegard of Bingen

The Peace

We stand

If it is possible, so far as it depends on you, live peaceably
with all.

The peace of the greening God,
the peace of Jesus, life of every life,
the peace of the Holy Spirit, energy of creation, be with you.
The peace of the Lord be always with you,
and also with you.

We exchange a sign of God's peace

Blessing

Greening God,
bless our loving.
Life of every life,
bless our living.
Energy of creation,
bless our changing.
The blessing of God,
Father, Son and Holy Spirit,
be with you now and for ever.
Amen.

Hymn/Song/Chant – *suggestions*

Lo, he comes with clouds descending

Here in this place (Gather us in)

Restore, O Lord

The Child Who is to Come

Advent pilgrimage

Introduction

These sections could be used separately over the four weeks of Advent, perhaps as the Ministry of the Word in a Eucharist, with a single visual focus each time, that would build up from week to week. If you prefer an Advent service to stand alone, two of the sections would work well together, perhaps Hoping and Waiting or Fearing and Preparing. All four sections could be used together as the basis of an Advent quiet morning or day. This could take the form of a pilgrimage around the church. Depending on your setting and the number of people taking part, there could be four different 'stations' around the church; or the people could remain static and the 'station' focus be brought to a central point. You might like to invite groups of people to create the 'stations', with the following focus:

1 **Hoping** Set up a cross. Prepare enough narrow yellow and purple ribbons for everyone to tie one of each to the cross. If there are large numbers you may like to tie each ribbon into a loop in advance, so they can be more easily hung.
2 **Waiting** A large central candle.
3 **Fearing** A sand tray or candle stand that will safely hold enough candles for each person to come forward and light one.
4 **Preparing** Pieces of paper and pens, enough for everyone.

A CELEBRATION OF ADVENT

Gathering Music – *suggestion*

Spiegel im spiegel – Arvo Pärt

Welcome

These four weeks of Advent are leading us towards the birth of a unique child. You are invited to share in this journey. Like parents anticipating the birth of their first-born child, we share in their hoping, their waiting, their fears, and their preparations.

Hymn/Song/Chant – *suggestions*

Make way! Make way!

Longing for light (Christ, be my light)

Light of the world

During this time we move to, or turn to, the first station

FIRST STATION

Hoping

Prayer

God of our deepest longing,
all our hopes are met in you.
You hear our heart's cry,
you know our deepest need.
Meet us in this place,
speak to us through the silence,
touch us with your healing love,
that we may share your hopes for the whole creation,
in and through Jesus, the child who is to come.
Amen.

Voice 1   I am Mary, still to be married, young, full of dreams
of husband and family, home-building, contentment
– that's my hope. But now, how can this be, that I
should be the handmaid of the Lord? 'Let it be to me
according to your word.'

Voice 2   I am Joseph, worked hard all my life, dreamed of a
son to follow me in the trade, a family business. But
with this news of a child not my own, I feel troubled,
ashamed, uncertain. Should I put her away, start again,
or swallow my pride? I feel like Job: 'Where then is my
hope? Who will see my hope?' (Job 17.15).

Voice 3   We are Israel, we have hoped for so long, dreamed of
           a coming saviour, promised by the prophets of old.
           We have lost our way, broken our covenant, lost our
           land and our freedom. We heard the prophet Isaiah
           promise: 'Look, the young woman is with child and
           shall bear a son, and shall name him Immanuel' (Isaiah
           7.14). Could God be with us?

Voice 4   What does God hope for? For our healing? For our
           love? For our returning? Listen to the word of the Lord
           in Jeremiah:

           For surely I know the plans I have for you, says the
           Lord, plans for your welfare and not for harm, to give
           you a future with hope. Then when you call upon me
           and come and pray to me, I will hear you. When you
           search for me, you will find me; if you seek me with all
           your heart, I will let you find me, says the Lord, and I
           will restore your fortunes and gather you from all the
           nations and all the places where I have driven you, says
           the Lord, and I will bring you back to the place from
           which I sent you into exile. (Jeremiah 29.11–14)

Reflection

In this time of reflection, let us bring our hopes to God. So what
do you hope for? What are your dreams? Do you feel as though
you have 'a future with hope'? Or do you feel betrayed, disappointed, hope-less? Have your hopes been dashed?

   Let us open ourselves to God and seek God with all our heart,
confident that God will hear us.

We take a purple ribbon and hold it, letting it symbolize our
hopelessness – in the quietness we name in our hearts where we
feel hopeless, anxious, afraid.
(Hold a few moments of silence)

We take a yellow ribbon and hold it, letting it symbolize for us our hope – in the quietness we name in our hearts where we feel hopeful, excited, alive.
(Hold a few moments of silence)

Music for Reflection – *suggestion*

Pavan – William Byrd

Response

As the music plays, we come forward to tie our ribbons to the cross, offering the whole of ourselves to God

Chant – *suggestion*

Bless the Lord, my soul (Taizé)

Prayers of Recognition

We bring to God all that feels hopeless in us,
our disappointments, our regrets;
and hold them in the light of God's assurance,
for us and for all creation.
(Silence)

No one who hopes in you
will ever be put to shame.

We bring to God all that is hopeful in us,
our dreams and aspirations;
and hold them in the light of God's hopes
for us and all creation.
(Silence)

No one who hopes in you
will ever be put to shame.

Hope of the world, as you called Mary to share your hopes
   and dreams,
may we respond with her:
Let it be with me according to your word.

Hope of the hopeless, as you called Joseph
beyond his disappointment,
may we respond with him:
Let it be with me according to your word.

Hope of all the nations, as you look in sorrow
at what we have become,
may we all respond:
Let it be with me according to your word.
Amen.

Hymn/Song/Chant – *suggestions*

   Tell out, my soul

   The angel Gabriel

   Magnificat (Taizé)

During this song we move to, or turn to, the second station

SECOND STATION

Waiting

Prayer

God of all time and eternity,
every moment of our lives is held in you.
You call us to be still and to wait with you.
Meet us in this place,
speak to us through the silence,
touch us with your healing love,
that we may rise up on eagles' wings,
in and through Jesus, the child who is to come.
Amen.

Voice 1   I am the voice of a mother, waiting nine months for the time to be completed, for the time to be right. My baby grows slowly, unseen: there is not much I can do but wait! As the psalmist says, 'Be still before the Lord, and wait patiently for him' (Psalm 37.7).

Voice 2   I am the voice of impatience: 'Buy now, pay later, instant credit, next-day delivery, why wait, you know you are worth it!' Why wait when you can have it now?

Voice 3   I am the voice of the desperate: 'How long, O Lord? Will you forget me for ever? How long will you hide your face from me? How long must I bear pain in my soul, and have sorrow in my heart all day long?' (Psalm 13.1–2).

Voice 4 Hear the voice of the Lord: 'Those who wait for the Lord shall renew their strength, they shall mount up with wings like eagles, they shall run and not grow weary, they shall walk and not faint' (Isaiah 40.31).

Reflection

The run-up to Christmas has become a time of frenetic activity that can leave us exhausted and jaded, full of stress and not at all ready to welcome the coming of Jesus. There are fewer opportunities to be still, to reflect, to wait on the Lord, to renew our strength. So now we are going to light a candle to help us hold a time of silence – to allow our bodies to be still, to allow our minds to be still, to allow God time to speak in our hearts. After the chant we shall hold five minutes of silence. You might like to use a repeated phrase to still your thoughts: 'Be still and know that I am God.'

A large candle is lit and placed centrally

Chant – *suggestion*

Wait for the Lord (Taizé)

Silence (about five minutes)

'Be still and know that I am God.'

Chant – *suggestion*

Wait for the Lord (Taizé)

Prayers for Recognition

We bring to God our busyness,
all that is frenetic, all that is jaded, all that is exhausted in us.
(Silence)

Wait for the Lord.
Keep watch, take heart.

We bring to God our impatience,
our frustrations and our unhappiness.
(Silence)

Wait for the Lord.
Keep watch, take heart.

We bring to God all that we are waiting for.
(Silence)

Wait for the Lord.
Keep watch, take heart.

> Be patient, therefore, beloved, until the coming of the Lord. The
> farmer waits for the precious crop from the earth, being patient
> with it until it receives the early and the late rains. (James 5.7)

Holy Spirit of God, we wait for you.
Speak to us with your still small voice of calm.
Renew our strength, restore our faith, refresh our vision.
Help us to wait for you through these weeks of Advent,
to make space,
to welcome the Word made flesh,
Jesus the child who is to come.
Amen.

Hymn/Song/Chant – *suggestions*

Dear Lord and Father of mankind

Be thou my vision

Come, thou long expected Jesus

In the Lord I'll be ever thankful (Taizé)

During this song we move, or turn, to the next station

THIRD STATION

Fearing

God of perfect love,
you help us to face our fears,
to know the truth about ourselves,
to be set free to grow and change.
You call us not to be afraid.
Meet us in this place,
speak to us through the silence,
touch us with your healing love,
that we may know you,
in and through Jesus, the child who is to come.
Amen.

Voice 1   I am Mary, I have to go far from home to be registered. I am so unsure, I fear the pain: will I know what to do, how to cope? Who will help me?

Voice 2   I am Joseph. Where will we stay? Soldiers everywhere, crowds, officials, counting, always counting. Who would bring a child into this fearful world?

Voice 3   I am John, the beloved disciple. The child who is to come taught us not to be afraid.
          Beloved, let us love one another, because love is from God; everyone who loves is born of God and knows God. Whoever does not love does not know God, for God is love. God's love was revealed among us in this way: God sent his only Son into the world so that we might live through him. In this is love, not that we

loved God but that he loved us and sent his Son to be the atoning sacrifice for our sins. Beloved, since God loved us so much, we also ought to love one another. No one has ever seen God; if we love one another, God lives in us, and his love is perfected in us.

By this we know that we abide in him and he in us, because he has given us of his Spirit. And we have seen and do testify that the Father has sent his Son as the Saviour of the world. God abides in those who confess that Jesus is the Son of God, and they abide in God. So we have known and believe the love that God has for us.

God is love, and those who abide in love abide in God, and God abides in them. Love has been perfected among us in this: that we may have boldness on the day of judgement, because as he is, so are we in this world. There is no fear in love, but perfect love casts out fear. (1 John 4.7–18)

Reflection

Jesus' first words to people were often, 'Do not be afraid', because he knew that we are so full of fears and worries. We fear for the future, for the unknown, for change, for ourselves, for our world. Today we recognize all that makes us fearful, and lift it in our prayers to the one who is perfect love, who will cast out our fear and give us peace. In the darkness of our fear we shall light a candle of perfect love. You are invited to come forward at any time to light your candle, to shine the light of perfect love on our human fear.

Candles are lit – you are invited to come forward to light a candle

Prayers of Intercession

Chant – *suggestion*

Don't be afraid (Wild Goose Worship)

For all who are fearful for the future,
for mothers bringing children into a fearful world,
for refugees and those caught up in conflict.
Don't be afraid ...

For all who are fearful for their health,
of growing older, of losing independence,
for those who are becoming confused, those awaiting test results.
Don't be afraid ...

For all who are fearful in an uncertain world of work,
of unemployment or redundancy,
of how to make ends meet and pay the bills.
Don't be afraid ...

For all who are fearful in relationships,
or of being alone and uncared for,
for those who are unhappy and feeling trapped.
Don't be afraid ...

God of perfect love,
cast out the fears that overshadow our lives.
Light of love, push back the darkness that hems us in,
that we may walk with confidence,
even into an uncertain future,
even in a fearful world,
with and through the child who is to come, Christ Jesus.
Amen.

Our Father, who art in heaven,
hallowed be thy name;
thy kingdom come,
thy will be done,
on earth as it is in heaven.

Give us this day our daily bread.
And forgive us our trespasses,
as we forgive those who trespass against us.
And lead us not into temptation,
but deliver us from evil.
For thine is the kingdom, the power, and the glory,
for ever and ever.
Amen.

Hymn/Song/Chant – *suggestions*

Do not be afraid, for I have redeemed you

Father, I place into your hands

During this song we move, or turn, to the next station

FOURTH STATION

Preparing

Prayer

Gracious God,
you prepare a way in the wilderness,
a table for our sustenance,
good things for our journeying.
You call us to prepare a way in our hearts.
Meet us in this place,
speak to us through the silence,
touch us with your healing love,
that we may prepare our lives for change,
in and through Jesus, the child who is to come.
Amen.

Voice 1   I am Mary. My time is closer now, I feel the movement
within me. Like countless mothers before me I feel the
need to prepare, to clear out, to make ready, full of
energy: they call it the nesting impulse. The Psalmist
speaks for me again, 'How great is your goodness
which you have prepared for those who love you'
(Psalm 31.19).

Voice 2   I am Isaiah and I speak for all those who have been waiting and hoping for change: all those who have been overlooked, downtrodden, forgotten.

Comfort, O comfort my people,
says your God.
Speak tenderly to Jerusalem,
and cry to her
that she has served her term,
that her penalty is paid,
that she has received from the Lord's hand
double for all her sins.
A voice cries out:
'In the wilderness prepare the way of the Lord,
make straight in the desert a highway for our God.
Every valley shall be lifted up,
and every mountain and hill be made low;
the uneven ground shall become level,
and the rough places a plain.
Then the glory of the Lord shall be revealed,
and all people shall see it together,
for the mouth of the Lord has spoken.'
(Isaiah 40.1–5)

Voice 3   I am John the Baptist. And long years after, I repeated those words: 'I am ... the voice of one crying in the wilderness: "Prepare the way of the Lord"' (Mark 1.3), as I called people to the waters of change. Who will listen? Who will come? Who will dare? What needs to change in your life? What will you leave behind to make room for God?

Voice 4   I am Paul. Remember that we are not alone in this. It is not just us, but God himself who prepares a way for us: 'No eye has seen, nor ear heard, nor the human heart conceived, what God has prepared for those who love him' (1 Corinthians 2.9).

Reflection

All the Christmas preparations seem to be about buying more stuff! But preparing the way of the Lord has to start with us, looking at our priorities. What is taking our time and energy? What fills our days? What are we worried about? Advent can be a time to declutter, to simplify, to clear out our lives and make room for God to grow in us. John the Baptist challenges us. What do you want to clear out, leave behind, be rid of? What do you want to change, to be different in your life after today?

You are invited to go off into the church to find a quiet corner, your own bit of wilderness. Take with you a sheet of paper and a pen, and make two lists – for yourself, not for anyone else. First, write down what you would like to leave behind, clear out, let go of; and second, write down what you would like to do differently, to take on, to change in your life. We will play some music for about five minutes; and we'll come back together when the chant begins.

Music – *suggestion*

Mass for four voices: Agnus Dei – William Byrd

Chant – *suggestion*

The kingdom of God is justice and peace (Taizé)

Prayers of Recognition

We offer to God our commitment to change,
to be different from this moment,
to prepare our hearts to meet him.
Prepare the way of the Lord.
Make his paths straight.

We offer to God all that we would clear out,
simplify and leave behind,
to prepare our hearts to meet him.
Prepare the way of the Lord.
Make his paths straight.

We offer to God all that we would become,
our energy, our imagination,
to prepare our hearts to meet him.
Prepare the way of the Lord.
Make his paths straight.

God of constancy and change,
Help us to recognize where we have become stuck
in the ruts of our familiar lives.
Break through our tired repetitions and jaded responses.
Prepare your way in us, make our paths straight,
that we might welcome your Son,
Jesus, the child who is to come.
Amen.

Blessing

God in our hoping,
strength in our waiting,
love in our fearing,
peace in our preparing,
be now among us,
child who is coming,
bring us your blessing,
now and always.
Amen.

Hymn/Song/Chant – *suggestions*

Sing to God

Through all the changing scenes of life

Will you come and follow me?

Bless the Lord, my soul (Taizé)

Locusts and Wild Honey

Celebrating acts of prophetic courage

Introduction

This could be a single service for Advent, or used in four parts throughout the Advent season. In a time when people want to be involved in discussing ideas or reflecting on their faith rather than simply listening to a sermon, this service offers the opportunity to turn faith into action. If possible people could gather in small groups of two or three for the discussion sections, choosing to sit with people they know less well, or from a different background. This could take place in a café style around tables, or simply in pews.

A CELEBRATION OF PROPHETIC COURAGE FOR ADVENT

Hymn/Song/Chant – *suggestions*

On Jordan's bank

The kingdom of God is justice and joy

Men of faith, rise up and sing

Welcome and Introduction

John the Baptist lived a life of prophetic courage and called us to prepare the way of the Lord. He spoke out fearlessly, challenging corruption, immorality and injustice. His appearance and his way of life, speaking from the margins, challenged others and attracted many to turn their lives around, coming for baptism in the river Jordan. Today we come to listen to that same voice of challenge, to find that same courage to change.

WELCOME THE STRANGER

Prayer

Wilderness God,
unfamiliar, unrecognized, unexpected,
find your home in us.
Shake our comfortable assumptions,
awaken us to your strangeness,
stretch us in new ways,
of being, of becoming, of belonging,
in the company of strangers.
Amen.

Reading – *Mark 1.1–8*

The beginning of the good news of Jesus Christ, the Son of God.
As it is written in the prophet Isaiah,

'See, I am sending my messenger ahead of you,
who will prepare your way;
the voice of one crying out in the wilderness:
"Prepare the way of the Lord,
make his paths straight"',

John the baptizer appeared in the wilderness, proclaiming a baptism of repentance for the forgiveness of sins. And people from the whole Judean countryside and all the people of Jerusalem were going out to him, and were baptized by him in the river Jordan, confessing their sins. Now John was clothed with camel's hair, with a leather belt around his waist, and he ate locusts and wild honey. He proclaimed, 'The one who is more powerful than I is coming after me; I am not worthy to stoop down and untie the thong of his sandals. I have baptized you with water; but he will baptize you with the Holy Spirit.'

Reflection

John was a stranger, living on the edge, in the margins of society. He looked different, dressed in camel skins; he lived a different life, eating locusts and wild honey. John was a wild man who seemed to stand against everything conventional and respectable. Yet people found him strangely compelling, and they responded to his challenge to 'repent and be baptized'. The people of Israel had always been reminded by God that they were strangers in Egypt, and that they should therefore welcome the stranger. When Jesus talks of what makes a difference, he says, 'I was a stranger and you welcomed me' (Matthew 25.35).

Jesus challenges us to love the stranger, to reach across the barriers of difference, of language and culture, of religion and colour. It is an act of prophetic courage, in our increasingly fearful world, to reach out positively to welcome the stranger: it is counter-cultural, in a world where strangers are suspected, where we warn our children of stranger danger. So how are we to do it? In this time of discussion, turn to your neighbours and explore these questions.

Discussion – *(two–three people)*

- Have you been the stranger?
- Where do you encounter strangers?
- How do you feel when meeting people of a different culture or religion?
- What makes it difficult to get to know people who are very different from us?
- What one thing could we do to welcome the stranger?

Action

Can this conversation transform us?

Gathering the responses, we commit ourselves to take steps to welcome the stranger, to make the effort to reach out and bridge the differences

Prayers of Recognition

Where we have been unwelcoming, inhospitable, unfriendly,
help us to open our hearts, our circles of friendship, our
   wider community
to welcome the stranger.
Come, Lord Jesus, be our guest.
Come to us as friend and stranger.

Where we have become comfortable, closed, complacent,
help us to open our minds, our thinking, our understanding,
to welcome the unfamiliar.
Come, Lord Jesus, be our guest.
Come to us as friend and stranger.

Where we have become conventional, respectable, proud,
help us to open ourselves, our faith, our lives,
to welcome the unconventional.
Come, Lord Jesus, be our guest.
Come to us as friend and stranger.

Offering

We offer to you our willingness to change,
   to grow, to deepen our faith.
Hold us in your love
As we embrace the stranger.

We offer to you our practical action, to become
   more welcoming.
Hold us in your love
As we embrace the stranger.

We offer to you our commitment to stick at it.
Hold us in your love
As we embrace the stranger.

Hymn/Song/Chant – *suggestions*

Here we will welcome the friend and the stranger

Inspired by love and anger

A new commandment

FEED THE HUNGRY

Prayer

Wilderness God,
unfamiliar, unrecognized, unexpected,
find your home in us.
In our emptiness, feed us.
Awaken in us a hunger for you.
Enable us to share our bread
in the company of the hungry.
Amen.

Reading – *Psalm 146*

Praise the Lord!
Praise the Lord, O my soul!
I will praise the Lord as long as I live;
I will sing praises to my God all my life long.
Do not put your trust in princes,
in mortals, in whom there is no help.
When their breath departs, they return to the earth;
on that very day their plans perish.
Happy are those whose help is the God of Jacob,
whose hope is in the Lord their God,
who made heaven and earth,
the sea, and all that is in them;
who keeps faith for ever;
who executes justice for the oppressed;
who gives food to the hungry.
The Lord sets the prisoners free;
the Lord opens the eyes of the blind.

The Lord lifts up those who are bowed down;
the Lord loves the righteous.
The Lord watches over the strangers;
he upholds the orphan and the widow,
but the way of the wicked he brings to ruin.
The Lord will reign for ever,
your God, O Zion, for all generations.
Praise the Lord!

Reflection

We have a complex relationship with food. We have so much to eat that we struggle with obesity. We eat for comfort, because we feel empty at a deeper level than simple nutrients can satisfy. We live alongside those who go hungry, in our own neighbourhoods, and across a narrowing world. This stark awareness of fundamental inequality is hard to live with, and feeds our own confusion.

For Jesus there was no confusion: he told the parable of the sheep and the goats, calling us to respond to the simple practical needs of others. For him, there can be no faith without action! He invites people to share their bread, to become companions – the word 'companion' comes from the Latin *com* meaning 'with' and *panis* meaning 'bread'. Sharing bread, sharing food, brings a far deeper sharing which feeds both the giver and receiver.

Discussion *(two–three people)*

- Have you ever been really hungry?
- Where is there hunger locally? Is there a food bank, credit union or local charity meeting this need? How could we support and help?
- Where is there hunger globally? What can be done, short term and long term?
- What one thing could we do to feed the hungry?

Action

Can this conversation transform us?

Gathering the responses, we commit ourselves to feeding the hungry, locally and globally

Prayers of Recognition

Where our own emptiness, despite our plenty,
has made us unaware, indifferent, uncaring,
help us to open our hearts, our tables, our wallets,
to feed the hungry.
Come, Lord Jesus, be our guest.
Come to us in the company we keep.

Where we have become forgetful, cynical, disheartened
   about hunger,
help us to begin again,
to share what we have.
Come, Lord Jesus, be our guest.
Come to us in the company we keep.

Where we feel overwhelmed by human need,
come to us in our human story and light the fire of
   our compassion.
Come, Lord Jesus, be our guest.
Come to us in the company we keep.

Offering

We offer to you our willingness to change,
to grow, to deepen our faith.
Hold us in your love,
as we share our bread.
We offer to you our practical action, to feed the hungry.
Hold us in your love,
as we share our bread.
We offer to you our commitment to stick at it.
Hold us in your love,
as we share our bread.

Hymn/Song/Chant – *suggestions*

God's Spirit is in my heart

Heaven shall not wait

Break our hearts

CLOTHE THE NAKED

Prayer

Wilderness God,
unfamiliar, unrecognized, unexpected,
find your home in us.
In our nakedness, clothe us.
In our vulnerability, protect us.
May we give shelter, sanctuary, support,
to all who stumble and fall.
Amen.

Reading – *Matthew 25.31–46*

'When the Son of Man comes in his glory, and all the angels with
him, then he will sit on the throne of his glory. All the nations
will be gathered before him, and he will separate people one
from another as a shepherd separates the sheep from the goats,
and he will put the sheep at his right hand and the goats at the
left. Then the king will say to those at his right hand, "Come,
you that are blessed by my Father, inherit the kingdom prepared
for you from the foundation of the world; for I was hungry and
you gave me food, I was thirsty and you gave me something to
drink, I was a stranger and you welcomed me, I was naked and
you gave me clothing, I was sick and you took care of me, I was
in prison and you visited me." Then the righteous will answer
him, "Lord, when was it that we saw you hungry and gave you
food, or thirsty and gave you something to drink? And when
was it that we saw you a stranger and welcomed you, or naked
and gave you clothing? And when was it that we saw you sick
or in prison and visited you?" And the king will answer them,

"Truly I tell you, just as you did it to one of the least of these who are members of my family, you did it to me." Then he will say to those at his left hand, "You that are accursed, depart from me into the eternal fire prepared for the devil and his angels; for I was hungry and you gave me no food, I was thirsty and you gave me nothing to drink, I was a stranger and you did not welcome me, naked and you did not give me clothing, sick and in prison and you did not visit me." Then they also will answer, "Lord, when was it that we saw you hungry or thirsty or a stranger or naked or sick or in prison, and did not take care of you?" Then he will answer them, "Truly I tell you, just as you did not do it to one of the least of these, you did not do it to me." And these will go away into eternal punishment, but the righteous into eternal life.'

Reflection

In our highly sexualized society we are confused by nakedness, intimacy and vulnerability. Clothing carries so much more significance than its simple function for protection, covering and warmth. It conveys status, power, wealth, fashion and identity. We can find ourselves with huge wardrobes of clothing, often unused. What then does it mean today to clothe the naked?

In the simplest of terms, Jesus said, if you have two shirts, give one away. On the most basic level we have seen people bringing warm clothes to the asylum seekers washed up from the Mediterranean, or to people sleeping rough in our cities, needing a clean change of clothes. In a more nuanced way, street pastors meet vulnerable young people coming out of nightclubs and offer shoes and warm layers to clothe people comfortably, to help them to be able to get home safely.

Discussion *(two–three people)*

- When have you felt most vulnerable? How important are clothes for you?
- What do your clothes say about you?
- Have you got more clothes than you need? What do you do with them?
- What one thing could we do to clothe the naked?

Action

Can this conversation transform us?

Gathering the responses, we commit ourselves to take steps to clothe the naked, locally and globally

Prayers of Recognition

Where we have judged others for what they wear,
looking on external appearance and not on the person inside,
help us to see beneath the surface, to clothe the naked.
Come, Lord Jesus, be our guest.
Come to us in our nakedness.

Where we have covered our own vulnerability with power
or image,
help us to find that inner confidence that knows we are precious
in your sight.
Come, Lord Jesus, be our guest.
Come to us in our nakedness.

Where we see the vulnerability in others, help us to be gentle,
to give sanctuary, to clothe the naked.
Come, Lord Jesus, be our guest.
Come to us in our nakedness.

Offering

We offer to you our willingness to change,
   to grow, to deepen our faith.
Hold us in your love,
as we learn to look like you.
We offer to you our practical action, to clothe the naked.
Hold us in your love,
as we learn to look like you.
We offer to you our commitment to stick at it.
Hold us in your love,
as we learn to look like you.

Hymn/Song/Chant – *suggestions*

When God almighty came to earth

Rock of ages

When I needed a neighbour

VISIT THE PRISONER

Prayer

Wilderness God,
unfamiliar, unrecognized, unexpected,
find your home in us.
When we are shut in by our fears,
open the gates of our hearts to your love.
May we bring hope to those who are imprisoned,
to all who long to be free.
Amen.

Reading – *Matthew 14.3–12*

> For Herod had arrested John, bound him, and put him in prison
> on account of Herodias, his brother Philip's wife, because
> John had been telling him, 'It is not lawful for you to have
> her.' Though Herod wanted to put him to death, he feared
> the crowd, because they regarded him as a prophet. But when
> Herod's birthday came, the daughter of Herodias danced before
> the company, and she pleased Herod so much that he promised
> on oath to grant her whatever she might ask. Prompted by her
> mother, she said, 'Give me the head of John the Baptist here on
> a platter.' The king was grieved, yet out of regard for his oaths
> and for the guests, he commanded it to be given; he sent and
> had John beheaded in the prison. The head was brought on a
> platter and given to the girl, who brought it to her mother. His
> disciples came and took the body and buried it; then they went
> and told Jesus.

Reflection

What are prisons for? For some they are places of punishment and deterrence; for others places of education and reform. John the Baptist was imprisoned to shut him up, for being critical of Herod's marriage. Many today are imprisoned for the same reason – prisoners of conscience are shut away for daring to criticize the authorities. But thousands of people are sent to prison because they have broken the law. Jesus didn't distinguish between those who were justly or unjustly imprisoned. So why should we be visiting people in prison? Jesus asks us not to forget people, not to write them off as irredeemable, but to keep them in mind, to keep in contact, to keep the connection of hope. Prisons can be brutalizing, damaging, schools of crime; but they have the potential to be humanizing, healing, places of reform. Our visit, our connection, may make that difference.

Discussion *(two–three people)*

- Have you ever felt imprisoned or trapped in a situation?
- Have you known anyone in prison, or visited a prison?
- How could we get involved with prisoners, or their families?
- Do you know anyone who is living in their own home, but still feels imprisoned?
- What one thing could we do to visit the prisoner?

Action

Can this conversation transform us?

Gathering the responses, we commit ourselves to visiting the prisoner, locally and globally

Prayers of Recognition

Where we have wanted revenge and punishment,
and forgotten the possibility of reform and healing,
help us never to give up on people,
to visit those in prison.
Come, Lord Jesus, be our guest.
Come to us when we are imprisoned.

Where we have taken our freedom for granted
and forgotten prisoners of conscience,
help us to use our freedom to press for theirs,
to visit those in prison.
Come, Lord Jesus, be our guest.
Come to us when we are imprisoned.

Where we see people imprisoned in their own homes
through fear or isolation, through challenges or disability,
help us to keep connected,
to visit those in prison.
Come, Lord Jesus, be our guest.
Come to us when we are imprisoned.

Offering

We offer to you our willingness to change,
to grow, to deepen our faith.
Hold us in your love.
Free us to use our freedom.
We offer to you our practical action,
to visit the prisoner.
Hold us in your love.
Free us to use our freedom.
We offer to you our commitment to stick at it.
Hold us in your love.
Free us to use our freedom.

Hymn/Song/Chant – *suggestions*

Amazing Grace

I will change your name

Make me a channel of your peace

Blessing

Wilderness God,
awaken compassion in us,
provoke courage in us,
arouse commitment in us,
nurture our thoughtful response
to all that is unjust.
Bless us now with the energy of your love,
Father, Son and Spirit.
Amen.

CHRISTMAS

Down to Earth

A carol service discovering the incarnation in our ordinary lives

Introduction

This service is based on the format of the traditional nine lessons and carols, but using some alternative readings to unfold a developing theme around the incarnation, kenosis, and our response. As it stands it will take about one and a quarter hours, depending on the music chosen, but could be reduced by taking out one or more sections. In a choral setting, choir anthems could be inserted instead of carols at various places.

Carol – *suggestions*

Once in royal David's city

O come, all ye faithful

Welcome and Introduction

We come to open our hearts and minds to the mystery of God born as a child in Bethlehem. Through our readings, prayers and carols, we will trace the loving purposes of God who comes in humility, laying aside all majesty and power. We will hear of Jesus who shows us the human face of God, who emptied himself for us, taking the form of a servant. We will listen to the Holy Spirit who invites us to see the presence of God in every human face and in the whole of creation.

Opening Prayer

God, you stoop to reach for us,
you give everything for us;
longing for our peace,
our fulfilment, our joy,
you give your very self.
Plumbing the depths of human darkness,
bringing your light,
you come in person
as the child in a manger.
Word made flesh,
God with us,
incarnate Love,
we open our lives, our hearts, our minds.
Show us how to see and love you
in Jesus, and in every human face.
Amen.

Anthem

IMAGE OF THE INVISIBLE GOD

It is beyond our imagination to picture the creator of the immensity of the cosmos. How can our finite minds picture the infinite? But the child at the heart of the Christmas story shows us the love of God on a human scale.

First Lesson – *Colossians 1.15–20*

Jesus shows us the human face of God.

He is the image of the invisible God, the firstborn of all creation; for in him all things in heaven and on earth were created, things visible and invisible, whether thrones or dominions or rulers or powers – all things have been created through him and for him. He himself is before all things, and in him all things hold together. He is the head of the body, the church; he is the beginning, the firstborn from the dead, so that he might come to have first place in everything. For in him all the fullness of God was pleased to dwell, and through him God was pleased to reconcile to himself all things, whether on earth or in heaven, by making peace through the blood of his cross.

Prayer

Child of the manger,
image of the invisible God,
fullness of all that is Love,
touch us now with your deep peace,
that we may be reconciled,
with you and with one another,
both on earth and in heaven,
as you give yourself completely,
for us.
Amen.

Carol – *suggestions*

See amid the winter snow

DELIGHTING IN THE HUMAN RACE

How do we picture God? Distant? Angry? Judging? There's lots of that in the Old Testament! But there are many other images too that we may be less familiar with. There are pictures of God as a nursing mother, or as an eagle caring for her chicks. In this reading, the picture is of a feminine Wisdom, collaborating with God in the process of creation, delighting in the human race.

Second Lesson – *Proverbs 8.22–31*

Holy Wisdom shows us that God delights in the human race.

The Lord created me at the beginning of his work,
the first of his acts of long ago.
Ages ago I was set up,
at the first, before the beginning of the earth.
When there were no depths I was brought forth,
when there were no springs abounding with water.
Before the mountains had been shaped,
before the hills, I was brought forth –
when he had not yet made earth and fields,
or the world's first bits of soil.
When he established the heavens, I was there,
when he drew a circle on the face of the deep,
when he made firm the skies above,
when he established the fountains of the deep,
when he assigned to the sea its limit,
so that the waters might not transgress his command,
when he marked out the foundations of the earth,
then I was beside him, like a master worker;

and I was daily his delight,
rejoicing before him always,
rejoicing in his inhabited world
and delighting in the human race.

Prayer

Child of the manger,
firstborn of all creation,
rejoicing in our diversity,
delighting in our humanity,
longing for our love,
touch us now with your joy,
with fullness of life,
as you give yourself completely,
for us.
Amen.

Carol – *suggestions*

Joy to the world

Christians, awake

A CHILD HAS BEEN BORN FOR US

God calls us to fullness of life, abundant life, but we continue to make choices that mean we walk in darkness, sorrow and pain. We live in a world of deep darkness where all can sometimes seem hopeless; but a child has been born for us, to be a light, to bring peace, to bring healing.

Third Lesson – *Isaiah 9.2–7*

In the face of human cruelty, a child shows us the true nature of God's peace.

The people who walked in darkness have seen a great light;
those who lived in a land of deep darkness—
on them light has shined.
You have multiplied the nation, you have increased its joy;
they rejoice before you as with joy at the harvest,
as people exult when dividing plunder.
For the yoke of their burden,
and the bar across their shoulders,
the rod of their oppressor,
you have broken as on the day of Midian.
For all the boots of the tramping warriors
and all the garments rolled in blood
shall be burned as fuel for the fire.
For a child has been born for us,
a son given to us;
authority rests upon his shoulders;
and he is named Wonderful Counsellor, Mighty God,
Everlasting Father, Prince of Peace.

His authority shall grow continually,
and there shall be endless peace
for the throne of David and his kingdom.
He will establish and uphold it
with justice and with righteousness
from this time onward and for evermore.
The zeal of the Lord of hosts will do this.

Prayer

Child of the manger,
Wonderful Counsellor,
Prince of Peace,
born for us,
in the face of violence and terror,
touch us now with your love,
your healing power,
as you give yourself completely,
for us.
Amen.

Carol – *suggestions*

In the bleak midwinter

Silent night

EMPTIED HIMSELF

We have traditionally pictured God as being all-powerful, unmoved and distant; but in the Christmas story we see God pouring himself into our humanity, to reach out to us. Jesus showed us that love is about emptying ourselves of power, giving ourselves utterly.

Fourth Lesson – *Philippians 2.5–11*

In coming as a child, God empties himself, gives himself utterly for us.

Let the same mind be in you that was in Christ Jesus,
who, though he was in the form of God,
did not regard equality with God
as something to be exploited,
but emptied himself,
taking the form of a slave,
being born in human likeness.
And being found in human form,
he humbled himself
and became obedient to the point of death –
even death on a cross.
Therefore God also highly exalted him
and gave him the name
that is above every name,
so that at the name of Jesus
every knee should bend,
in heaven and on earth and under the earth,
and every tongue should confess

that Jesus Christ is Lord,
to the glory of God the Father.

Prayer

Child of the manger,
vulnerable, needy, helpless,
God's love made human,
word made flesh,
touch us now with your gentleness,
your humility,
as you give yourself completely,
for us.
Amen.

Carol – *suggestions*

Unto us is born a Son

Of the Father's love begotten

LET IT BE WITH ME

God has created us to be free, and accords us the dignity of choice, inviting us to cooperate in creation. In reaching out to us, God relies on our response, standing at the door, but waiting for our invitation. Without Mary's willing acceptance, God can do nothing. So her availability to God is vital, to allow Jesus to be born: Mary opens herself to God when she says, 'Let it be with me according to your word.'

Fifth Lesson – *Luke 1.26–38*

God works with us to overcome our fears, to allow us to become part of his life.

In the sixth month the angel Gabriel was sent by God to a town in Galilee called Nazareth, to a virgin engaged to a man whose name was Joseph, of the house of David. The virgin's name was Mary. And he came to her and said, 'Greetings, favoured one! The Lord is with you.' But she was much perplexed by his words and pondered what sort of greeting this might be. The angel said to her, 'Do not be afraid, Mary, for you have found favour with God. And now, you will conceive in your womb and bear a son, and you will name him Jesus. He will be great, and will be called the Son of the Most High, and the Lord God will give to him the throne of his ancestor David. He will reign over the house of Jacob for ever, and of his kingdom there will be no end.' Mary said to the angel, 'How can this be, since I am a virgin?' The angel said to her, 'The Holy Spirit will come upon you, and the power of the Most High will overshadow you; therefore, the child to be born will be holy; he will be called Son of God. And now, your relative Elizabeth in her old age has also conceived a son; and this is the sixth month for her who was said to be barren. For nothing will be impossible with God.' Then Mary said, 'Here am I, the servant of the Lord; let it be with me according to your word.' Then the angel departed from her.

Prayer

Child of the manger,
overshadowing of the Most High,
impossible hope made possible,
Son of God,
incarnate Love,
touch us now with your open invitation,
enable us to respond,
as you give yourself completely,
for us.
Amen.

Carol – *suggestions*

The angel Gabriel

It came upon the midnight clear

MESS AND MUDDLE

So much could go wrong. Human systems, power struggles, indifference. Life is cheap and birth is dangerous. God risked everything in reaching out to us, in coming as a child into the mess and muddle of our real lives. God invites us to do the same, to risk everything for love.

Sixth Lesson – *Luke 2.1–7*

God risks all for love, and comes into the mess and muddle of our lives.

> In those days a decree went out from Emperor Augustus that all the world should be registered. This was the first registration and was taken while Quirinius was governor of Syria. All went to their own towns to be registered. Joseph also went from the town of Nazareth in Galilee to Judea, to the city of David called Bethlehem, because he was descended from the house and family of David. He went to be registered with Mary, to whom he was engaged and who was expecting a child. While they were there, the time came for her to deliver her child. And she gave birth to her firstborn son and wrapped him in bands of cloth, and laid him in a manger, because there was no place for them in the inn.

Prayer

Child of the manger,
born into the mess and muddle
of faceless, uncaring bureaucracy,
experiencing closing of doors, shutting of minds,
risking all for love of us,
touch us now with your profoundly simple presence,
as you give yourself completely,
for us.
Amen.

Carol – *suggestions*

Away in a manger

Infant holy

GOOD NEWS OF GREAT JOY

Religions tend to try to keep God bottled up, defined, controlled. But the Christmas story turns all this on its head, starting with a breaking of the boundaries. This good news is not just for a minority or an elite, not just for people who are religious or who have got life sorted out: it's for everyone, for all the people, even the night shift. God announces the coming Saviour to the shepherds.

Seventh Lesson – *Luke 2.8–12*

The sign of hope for the ordinary people and for everyone was something so familiar – a baby!

> In that region there were shepherds living in the fields, keeping watch over their flock by night. Then an angel of the Lord stood before them, and the glory of the Lord shone around them, and they were terrified. But the angel said to them, 'Do not be afraid; for see – I am bringing you good news of great joy for all the people: to you is born this day in the city of David a Saviour, who is the Messiah, the Lord. This will be a sign for you: you will find a child wrapped in bands of cloth and lying in a manger.'

Prayer

Child of the manger,
Saviour, Messiah, sign of our freedom,
your birth broke down the barriers,
crossed every boundary,
included everyone,
giving good news for all the people.
Touch us now with your good news,
opening us to love that crosses boundaries,
as you give yourself completely,
for us.
Amen.

Carol – *suggestions*

While shepherds watched

The first noel

SEEING WHO WE REALLY ARE

The Christmas story is very familiar; it's comforting to hear it again. But what difference does it make? Will we be any different after returning to the Christmas story in this service? Will anything have changed for us? God became one of us in Jesus, to show us who we really are, as children of God, so that we can begin to recognize God in every human face. I wonder where we need to be surprised by recognizing God in others.

Eighth Lesson – *Mother Teresa of Calcutta*

God asks us to see Jesus in every human face, and to love them as we are loved.

> I believe in person to person. Every person is Christ for me, and since there is only one Jesus, that person is the one person in the world at that moment. I see Christ in every person I touch, it is as simple as that.

> Whenever I meet someone in need, it is really Jesus in his most distressing disguise.

> To be able to love one another, we must pray much, for prayer gives a clean heart and a clean heart can see God in our neighbour. If now we have no peace, it is because we have forgotten how to see God in one another. If each person saw God in his neighbour, do you think we would need guns and bombs?

Prayer

Child of the manger,
you are found in the hungry, lonely, lost.
We meet you in our friends and neighbours,
even in strangers or those we struggle with.
Help us to see your image,
the Word made flesh, in one another.
Touch us now with your compassion,
as you give yourself completely,
for us.
Amen.

Carol – *suggestions*

Good King Wenceslas

In the bleak midwinter

THE WORD BECAME FLESH

In Jesus, God comes close to us, bends to reach us, and empties himself, to become one of us. God invites us to recognize who we are, who other people are, and to share in the abundance of life and love that this unlocks.

Ninth Lesson – *John 1.1–14*

John unfolds the mystery of God becoming one of us, the Word made flesh:

> In the beginning was the Word, and the Word was with God, and the Word was God. He was in the beginning with God. All things came into being through him, and without him not one thing came into being. What has come into being in him was life, and the life was the light of all people. The light shines in the darkness, and the darkness did not overcome it.
>
> There was a man sent from God, whose name was John. He came as a witness to testify to the light, so that all might believe through him. He himself was not the light, but he came to testify to the light. The true light, which enlightens everyone, was coming into the world.
>
> He was in the world, and the world came into being through him; yet the world did not know him. He came to what was his own, and his own people did not accept him. But to all who received him, who believed in his name, he gave power to become children of God, who were born, not of blood or of the will of the flesh or of the will of man, but of God.
>
> And the Word became flesh and lived among us, and we have seen his glory, the glory as of a father's only son, full of grace and truth.

Prayer

Child of the manger,
life shining light
into the darkest places,
life for every one of us,
empower us to become
children of Light,
children of Love,
children of God.
Touch us now with your true light,
enable us to open ourselves to you,
as you give yourself completely,
for us.
Amen.

Carol – *suggestions*

A great and mighty wonder

O little town of Bethlehem

Responses

No one has ever seen God;
if we love one another,
God lives in us,
and his love is perfected in us.
God is love,
and those who live in love, live in God,
and God lives in them.
(1 John 4.12, 16)

Our Father, who art in heaven,
hallowed be thy name;
thy kingdom come,
thy will be done,
on earth as it is in heaven.
Give us this day our daily bread.
And forgive us our trespasses,
as we forgive those who trespass against us.
And lead us not into temptation,
but deliver us from evil.
For thine is the kingdom, the power, and the glory,
for ever and ever.
Amen.

Blessing

God who is fullness of Love,
dwell in our hearts.
Christ who holds all things together,
bring peace in our world.
Spirit who awakens us to life's mystery,
bring us your blessing,
now and always.
Amen.

Carol – *suggestions*

Hark, the herald angels sing

We're Included

A crib service celebrating the inclusive love of God

Introduction

In this crib service you can encourage the children attending to dress up in nativity costumes and take part in the service. You could adapt it to include tableaux of the nativity or drama scenes for each section. You will need an empty crib scene set up at the front. As the story unfolds, the nativity figures can be brought up, adding each one in turn during the service. It will be useful to have some authorized adult helpers to organize the logistics of this process to minimize the time taken. Have some spare costumes available if possible, for children who have not come already dressed up. In producing your order of service, it may be good to consider reducing the numbers of verses in the carols to help keep down the length of the service. Readings will work best if they are taken from a children's Bible, and are read by children.

Welcome

Carol – *suggestion*

Once in royal David's city

MARY IS INCLUDED

Who would you choose to be on your team? The fittest, the strong-est, or most popular people are often the ones who get chosen. But Mary was a very ordinary young woman, from a very ordinary town and family; she was nothing special – not the obvious choice for the dream team! And yet God chose her to be part of his plan. She would give birth to a baby who would change the world for everyone. She was included, to show we can all be included in God's loving plan.

Reading 1 – *Luke 1.26–38*

All those dressed as an Angel – come forward

Prayer

Loving God,
you chose Mary to be included,
to be mother of your child Jesus,
although she was from an ordinary town and family,
a young person.
We pray for ordinary people and
young people everywhere.
Help us to know that we are all included
in your loving plan,
to bring hope to our world.
Amen.

The figures of the animals are brought to the crib during this next carol

Carol – *suggestion*

The Virgin Mary had a baby boy

JOSEPH IS INCLUDED

What would your ideal family be? Mum, dad, two kids? Well, God chose a carpenter called Joseph to be in his family, to be part of his plan. Joseph was included, was needed, to help and support Mary, even though he wasn't Jesus' real dad. He was to be a stepfather for Jesus. He was included, showing that all sorts of family patterns can work, and that we can all be included in God's loving plan.

Reading 2 – *Luke 2.1–7*

All those dressed as Mary and Joseph or the donkey – come forward

Prayer

Loving God,
you chose Joseph to be included,
to be stepfather to your child Jesus.
We pray for all parents,
step-parents and adoptive parents,
for all patterns of family life.
Help us to know that we are all included
in your loving plan,
to bring hope to our world.
Amen.

The figures of Mary and Joseph are brought to the crib

Carol – *suggestion*

Little donkey

SHEPHERDS ARE INCLUDED

If you had good news, who would you tell it to first? Who would you invite to your party? Family, friends, neighbours? We often invite those closest to us. Well, God invited the least likely people to come to see Jesus. People we sometimes look down on. Shepherds from the fields, people used to living rough, working all night; these were to be the first visitors, to see God's plan unfolding. They were included, because even the people who often aren't noticed and valued are equally important to God, so that we can all be included in God's loving plan.

Reading 3 – *Luke 2.8–20*

All those dressed as shepherds – come forward

Prayer

Loving God,
you chose shepherds to be included,
rough sleepers, hard workers,
people often looked down on,
to welcome your child Jesus.
Help us to know that we are all included
in your loving plan,
to bring hope to our world.
Amen.

The figures of the shepherds are brought to the crib

Carol – *suggestion*

While shepherds watched

THE WISE MEN ARE INCLUDED

I wonder why the wise men were included. They were from a different country, even a different religion. They seemed to have nothing in common with Mary and Joseph. Why did God invite them to visit Jesus? Perhaps to show that God's plan was not just for us, not just for people like us, but for people we think of as strangers too, for everyone in the whole world. This child Jesus was to include everyone in God's loving plan.

Reading 4 – *Matthew 2.1–12*

Those dressed as wise men, kings and stars – all come forward

Prayer

Loving God,
you chose wise men from far away to be included,
foreigners, strangers,
people who seem so different from us,
to welcome your child Jesus.
Help us to know that we are all included
in your loving plan,
to bring hope to our world.
Amen.

The figures of the wise men are brought to the crib

Carol – *suggestion*

We three kings

YOU ARE INCLUDED

Lots of us have known what it's like not to be included, and sometimes to be left out. It can leave us feeling unwanted, unwelcome, unloved. But in the birth of Jesus we hear God saying to Mary, Joseph, the shepherds, the wise men, and also to every single one of us, 'You are included.' We don't have to do anything to earn our place in God's love. We are already there! This Christmas, God invites us all to see that we are included, and invites us simply to say, 'Yes!'

Reading – *John V. Taylor, 'To a Grandchild'*

Over the swinging parapet of my arm
your sentinel eyes lean gazing. Hugely alert
in the pale unfinished clay of your infant face,
they drink, light from this candle on the tree.
Drinking, not pondering, each bright thing you see,
you make it yours without analysis
and, stopping down the aperture of thought
to a fine pinhole, you are filled with flame.

Give me for Christmas, then, your kind of seeing,
not studying candles – angel, manger, star –
but staring as at a portrait, God's I guess,
that shocks and holds the eye, till all my being,
gathered, intent and still, as now you are,
breathes out its wonder in a wordless 'yes'.

At the end of our service you are invited to come to the crib, to take a moment for that kind of seeing, to lean gazing, drinking, not pondering, and to say your own 'yes': yes, you know that you are included in God's loving plan.

There is one figure missing from our crib – who is it?

The figure of the Christ child is brought to the crib

Prayer

Loving God,
you're happy to choose the most unlikely people to be included.
You choose the lowest, the least, the unloved,
the people who don't feel as though they deserve it,
to welcome your child Jesus.
Help us to know that we are all included
in your loving plan,
to bring hope to our world.
Amen.

Blessing

With the angels from heaven,
we are included!
With the shepherds, the last and the least,
we are included!
With the wise men, the different, the stranger,
we are included!
With Mary and Joseph, the ordinary, everyday folk,
we are included!
With the Christ child, laid in a manger,
we are included!

May God bless us and keep us,
included in his heart of love;
may we recognize that we are included,
in God's loving purposes for our world,
so that we join wholeheartedly,
with the whole of creation,
offering our wordless 'yes'.
Amen.

Carol – *suggestion*

O come, all ye faithful

Martyr, Exile, Victim

Darkness in the Christmas season

Introduction

This material can either be used as one service covering all the festivals, or in sections for each of the days after Christmas. Each could be used as the Ministry of the Word, as part of a Eucharist.

Hymn/Song/Chant – *suggestions*

What child is this?

Cloth for the cradle

In our darkness (Taizé)

Welcome

We have sometimes reduced the nativity to a saccharine-sweet fairytale of donkeys, innkeepers and tea-towelled shepherds. In these days after Christmas, we can recover some of the real life that has been obscured. Three feast days, easily overlooked, take us into the depths of struggle and suffering. Stephen, first martyr, stoned to death for his faith. John, exiled to the island of Patmos for his writing. The Holy Innocents, most cruelly of all, children murdered in Bethlehem in an attempt to destroy the Christ-child. As we reflect on human violence, oppression and terror, so we draw near to all who suffer today. We pray for justice for the oppressed, we pray for release for the captives, and we pray for peace for those who mourn.

STEPHEN

First martyr

Opening Responses

He was in the world,
and the world came into being through him;
yet the world did not know him.
He came to what was his own,
and his own people did not accept him.
Lord, have mercy upon us.
(John 1.10–11)

Opening Prayer

Word made flesh,
God with us,
child in a manger,
we are your own people
made in your image,
often struggling to know you,
sometimes failing to accept you.
We come to you now,
asking you to be with us as we dare to look deeper
into the mystery of your love
for us, and for all your children.
Amen.

Reading – *Acts 7.54–60*

We hear the story of Stephen, stoned to death as the first Christian martyr.

> When they heard these things, they became enraged and ground their teeth at Stephen. But filled with the Holy Spirit, he gazed into heaven and saw the glory of God and Jesus standing at the right hand of God. 'Look,' he said, 'I see the heavens opened and the Son of Man standing at the right hand of God!' But they covered their ears, and with a loud shout all rushed together against him. Then they dragged him out of the city and began to stone him; and the witnesses laid their coats at the feet of a young man named Saul. While they were stoning Stephen, he prayed, 'Lord Jesus, receive my spirit.' Then he knelt down and cried out in a loud voice, 'Lord, do not hold this sin against them.' When he had said this, he died.

Living Word of God,
speak within our hearts.

Silence

Reflection

Stephen had been selected to be a deacon, someone who would ensure that there was a fair distribution of welfare for the widows. He was tasked with caring for the poor, with making sure that the early Church practised what it preached. Before long he also started to speak publicly of his faith, and he was dragged before the religious authorities. What made them so angry, so enraged? Perhaps it was because Stephen challenged their comfortable certainties, their sense of control, their monopoly on God? Whenever we see such extremes of emotion, such a disproportionate reaction, we know that it points to a much deeper issue. When we feel something very strongly we need to ask ourselves why; what is really going on?

Music for Reflection – *suggestion*

Peter Grimes: Act 1, The Storm – Benjamin Britten

In the quietness after the music we think about what makes us most angry, the people we find it hardest to get along with, and the times we refuse to listen

Prayers of Recognition

We bring to God the things that enrage us,
the times we feel powerful anger;
and in the quietness we ask for grace,
to understand our deepest feelings,
our real motives.
(Silence)

May we see heaven opened.
Lord Jesus, receive my spirit.

We bring to God the times we cover our ears
and refuse to listen;
and in the quietness we ask for grace,
to understand our deepest feelings,
our real motives.
(Silence)

May we see heaven opened.
Lord Jesus, receive my spirit.

We bring to God the stones we throw,
the accusations we make,
the assumptions we project;
and in the quietness we ask for grace,
to understand our deepest feelings,
our real motives.
(Silence)

May we see heaven opened.
Lord Jesus, receive my spirit.

Prayers of Intercession

For all who are persecuted for their faith today,
Lord, hear us.
For all who speak out for freedom, justice and peace,
Lord, hear us.
For those who have been imprisoned, tortured, or killed,
Lord, hear us.
For those who have stood by and done nothing,
Lord, have mercy.

Collect
God in our courageous living,
God in our serving of others,
God in our speaking out,
help us to know that you live in us,
serve with us,
and speak through us.
For Stephen the martyr,
for all lives given or taken
for the cause of your kingdom,
may Love's resurrection
be fulfilled.
Amen.

Hymn/Song/Chant – *suggestions*

Ye watchers and ye holy ones

All hail the power of Jesus' name

JOHN

In exile

Opening Responses

In the beginning was the Word,
and the Word was with God,
and the Word was God.
He was in the beginning with God.
All things came into being through him,
and without him not one thing came into being.
(John 1.1–3)

Opening Prayer

Word made flesh,
God with us,
child in a manger,
from the beginning you have loved us,
you hold us in being, every moment of our lives,
you call us and shape us.
We come to you now,
asking you to be with us as we dare to look deeper
into the mystery of your love
for us, and for all your children.
Amen.

Reading – *Revelation 1.9; 13.5–7*

We hear John speaking and we hear the writing for which he was
exiled, when he compared the Roman Emperor to a beast.

I, John, your brother who share with you in Jesus the persecution and the kingdom and the patient endurance, was on the island called Patmos because of the word of God and the testimony of Jesus.

The beast was given a mouth uttering haughty and blasphemous words, and it was allowed to exercise authority for 42 months. It opened its mouth to utter blasphemies against God, blaspheming his name and his dwelling, that is, those who dwell in heaven. Also, it was allowed to make war on the saints and to conquer them.

Living Word of God,
speak within our hearts.

Silence

Reflection

Christians have traditionally identified St John the Evangelist, or gospel writer, with John who was Jesus' disciple and with John who wrote Revelation and was exiled to the island of Patmos. From the earliest times Christians were persecuted for their faith, not only by the religious authorities but by the Roman Empire, which tried to suppress them. It is thought that John was exiled to the island of Patmos because of his writing, especially the book of Revelation with its many coded references to those in power, like his references to the Roman Emperor as 'the beast'. In our own time, many people have been forced from their home lands into exile in a strange country. Today, when so many are displaced by war, or poverty, John's exile can connect us with their suffering and help us to respond. We too may know times of exile, when we feel we don't belong.

Music for Reflection – *suggestion*

Whirling Winds – Ludovico Einaudi

In the quietness we think about the times and places where we have felt we don't belong, where we are powerless, where we have been silenced.

Prayers of Recognition

We bring to God our own sense of exile,
our own displacement from home, family, work, health, peace,
where our values are dismissed or overturned,
where our faith is disregarded or ridiculed.
(Silence)

As we share with Jesus the persecution,
may we share the patient endurance of the kingdom.

We bring to God our own sense of powerlessness,
in the face of all that dictates our lives,
all who wield power without love,
all that oppresses, constrains and distorts.
(Silence)

As we share with Jesus the persecution,
may we share the patient endurance of the kingdom.

We bring to God the times we are silent and passive,
when we fail to speak out or take action,
when our faith is timid and fearful,
when we walk past on the other side.
(Silence)

Lord have mercy,
may we share the patient endurance of the kingdom.

Prayers of Intercession

For all who are in exile today,
Lord, hear us.
For all who have been silenced today,
Lord, hear us.
For those who are fleeing from war and poverty,
Lord, hear us.
For those who have stood by and done nothing,
Lord, have mercy.

Collect

God, in our exile,
God, in our silencing,
God, in our imprisonment,
help us to look to you,
to see through our losses
of freedom, of courage, of home,
to your kingdom within us.
For John the exile,
for all who are far from home
for the cause of your kingdom,
may Love's resurrection
be fulfilled.
Amen.

Hymn/Song/Chant – *suggestions*

Longing for light

Who is this, so weak and helpless

O Thou who camest from above

HOLY INNOCENT
Victim

Opening Responses

What has come into being in him was life,
and the life was the light of all people.
The light shines in the darkness,
and the darkness did not overcome it.
But to all who received him,
who believed in his name,
he gave power to become children of God.
(John 1.3–5, 12)

Opening Prayer

Word made flesh,
God with us,
child in a manger,
in the very darkest times,
when light and love and even life itself
is extinguished,
when all hope has gone,
you are still our light, our love, our life.
We come to you now,
asking you to be with us as we dare to look deeper,
into the mystery of your love
for us, and for all your children.
Amen.

Reading – *Matthew 2.16–18*

We hear of Herod's fury and his order to kill all the children in Bethlehem under two years of age.

> When Herod saw that he had been tricked by the wise men, he was infuriated, and he sent and killed all the children in and around Bethlehem who were two years old or under, according to the time that he had learned from the wise men. Then was fulfilled what had been spoken through the prophet Jeremiah:

> 'A voice was heard in Ramah,
> wailing and loud lamentation,
> Rachel weeping for her children;
> she refused to be consoled, because they are no more.'

Living Word of God,
speak within our hearts.

Silence

Reflection

The death of a child is devastating. The murder of a child is even worse. The destruction of helpless innocent lives, cut short when they have hardly begun, leaves parents paralysed with grief. Herod's order to wipe out all the little children in Bethlehem, in order to kill the child Jesus, to cut off all possible challengers to his power, is remembered as 'the slaughter of the innocents'. These children are called the 'Holy Innocents' – we could also say that they are wholly, or completely, innocent. In our own time, the slaughter of innocent lives is continuing: the malnutrition of millions of children the world over; the killing of children as part of ethnic cleansing in Bosnia and genocide in Rwanda; countless deaths in acts of terror in Syria; and other appalling stories of the murder of children. We sanitize our own part in this, using language like 'collateral damage', where in reality each dead child represents a life-changing loss. The loss ripples out from that unique, irreplaceable individual life, affecting the family, their community, our common humanity. We too must refuse to be consoled or to accept easy platitudes in the face of such loss. We must bring to God our outrage and our heartfelt desire for change.

Music for Reflection – *suggestions*

Lalalala Gohle Laleh, from Lullabies from the Axis of Evil

In the quietness we think about our own loss and grief, and the big news stories that move us – today's slaughtered innocents

Prayers of Recognition

We bring to God our own experience of loss,
the sadness of separation, the grief and tears we have known,
in solidarity with those who weep today.
(Silence)

Rachel weeping for her children.
Refusing to be consoled, because they are no more.

We bring to God our compassion fatigue,
in the face of so many stories in the news,
our sanitizing of slaughter,
the times we forget that these are all people like us.
(Silence)

Rachel weeping for her children.
Refusing to be consoled, because they are no more.

We bring to God some of the false consolations
we use to dull the edge of our grieving,
rejecting the distractions and oblivions we seek,
and opening ourselves instead to the healing gift of tears.
(Silence)

Rachel weeping for her children,
Refusing to be consoled, because they are no more.

Prayers of Intercession

For all who are grieving for their children today,
Lord, hear us.
For all who feel they have no future today,
Lord, hear us.
For those who have no one to tell,
Lord, hear us.
For those who have stood by and done nothing,
Lord, have mercy.

Collect

God in our frozen grieving,
God in our desperate weeping,
God in our isolation,
help us look to you,
not for consolation,
but for healing,
in your kingdom within us.
For the Holy Innocents,
for all who have been taken from us
for the cause of your kingdom,
may Love's resurrection
be fulfilled.
Amen.

Words of Hope

In a world of such cruelty and pain, we can feel overwhelmed by its darkness. But God promises us that the light shines in the darkness and the darkness has not overcome it. So we affirm confidently together the words written by Archbishop Desmond Tutu:

**Goodness is stronger than evil;
love is stronger than hate;
light is stronger than darkness;
life is stronger than death.**
(There is a sung version of this by John Bell)

We come to the heart of our faith in God, our confidence in the promise of resurrection life that leads us through death to life. We hear words of reassurance from the Bible, drawing deep from the reservoirs of hope that people have turned to over the centuries.

'I have said this to you, so that in me you may have peace. In the world you face persecution. But take courage; I have conquered the world!'
(John 16.33)

The Lord is near to the broken-hearted,
and saves the crushed in spirit.
(Psalm 34.18)

Though I walk in the midst of trouble,
you preserve me against the wrath of my enemies;
you stretch out your hand,
and your right hand delivers me.
The Lord will fulfil his purpose for me;
your steadfast love, O Lord, endures for ever.
Do not forsake the work of your hands.
(Psalm 138.7–8)

Blessing

God who so loves the world,
you give yourself utterly for us.
Bring us through our cruelty and inhumanity,
help us to turn our hearts,
to change our ways,
to make amends.

We commit ourselves to loving in your name,
fired by a vision
of how we can trust in your transforming love.
God who loves us,
Jesus who saves us,
Spirit who moves us,
bless us now.
Amen.

Hymn/Song/Chant – *suggestions*

O God of earth and altar

I will change your name

Empty, broken, here I stand (Kyrie eleison)

NEW YEAR

All Things New

Behold, I am making
all things new.
Revelation 21.5

Ring out the Old

A service to welcome the New Year

Introduction

At this pivotal point of the turning of the year, we are drawn both to look back at the year that is ending and look forward to the year ahead. This service to welcome the new year is based on the structure of the daily examen, devised 400 years ago by St Ignatius of Loyola. He developed a way of prayerful reflection, which looks back over the day just gone, and forward to the following. So we will take time, here, to reflect fully on the experiences of the year now ending, acknowledging some of the deep wisdom and learning of the past year and taking it forwards, to inform our living in the year to come.

Carol/Hymn/Song – *suggestion*

Lord, for the years

O God, our help in ages past

BECOMING AWARE OF GOD'S PRESENCE

Opening Responses

Lord, you have been our dwelling-place,
in all generations.
Before the mountains were brought forth,
before ever you had formed the earth and the world,
from everlasting to everlasting you are God.
For a thousand years in your sight
are like yesterday when it is past,
or like a watch in the night.
(Psalm 90.1–2, 4)

Preparation

God is present, whether we notice or not. We don't need to make God present, or pray for God to be present – God is present. It's just that we don't always realize it! In order to become aware of the presence of God, we need to recognize the things that preoccupy us, the things inside us and around us that distract us, the voices that divert our attention, the thoughts that intrude. It is important to name our heartfelt desire, to ask God, 'Let me be aware of your presence'; and then to wait expectantly for that awareness to grow. This is the work of our heart, not our intellect, so we need to follow our heart. It takes practice, so do not be discouraged if your mind wanders or thoughts intrude. But whenever that happens – as it surely will! – it can help to respond to the distraction with a simple word or phrase. When you notice your mind wandering, simply use a phrase such as, 'Be still and know that I am God', and let go of the stray thought.

Hymn/Song/Chant – *suggestions*

Be still, for the presence of the Lord

O breath of life, come sweeping through us

Laudate omnes gentes (Taizé)

Shared Silence *(about five minutes)*

As we hold a time of shared silence we hold this word or phrase in our hearts

Let me be aware of your presence.

REVIEWING THE PAST YEAR
WITH GRATITUDE

Reading – *Ecclesiastes 3.1–8*

For everything there is a season, and a time for every matter
   under heaven:
a time to be born, and a time to die;
a time to plant, and a time to pluck up what is planted;
a time to kill, and a time to heal;
a time to break down, and a time to build up;
a time to weep, and a time to laugh;
a time to mourn, and a time to dance;
a time to throw away stones, and a time to gather
   stones together;
a time to embrace, and a time to refrain from embracing;
a time to seek, and a time to lose;
a time to keep, and a time to throw away;
a time to tear, and a time to sew;
a time to keep silence, and a time to speak;
a time to love, and a time to hate;
a time for war, and a time for peace.

Living Word of God,
speak within our hearts.

Reflection

Some people never seem to look back or to dwell on past events;
they are always on to the next thing. Others find it hard to move
on, and can get stuck in the past.

At the turning of the year we take this time to review the past year with gratitude. It may have been a wonderful year, with happy memories coming to mind. It may have been a hard year, with painful experiences and memories. It may have been a mixture of joy and sorrow.

Paul encourages us to 'give thanks in all circumstances' (1 Thessalonians 5.18). Can we dare to adopt an 'attitude of gratitude', where we not only give thanks for the joys of the past year, but we also find a way to give thanks for all that we have learned through the challenging times we have experienced? This can take some doing when things have been tough, but it can be a powerful way of allowing us to move on when we have become stuck in a negative place, when we have been overwhelmed by pain or hurt or grief, to grow through and integrate even the most painful memories.

Music for Reflection – *suggestion*

Song for Athene (extract) – John Tavener

During this time think through the events of the past year: all that has happened in your life, and focus on the ups and downs. You may find it helpful to hold your hands open in front of you, as a sign of being open to any memories that flood in. Every time you remember something positive, look at one of your hands; every time you remember something that's tough, look at the other hand.

Prayer

God of every matter under heaven,
we offer the events and experiences of the past year,
in thankfulness for your presence with us,
through thick and thin.
We offer the whole of ourselves,
because you love the whole of ourselves.
Give us grace to leave these memories here,
safe in your arms of love.
Amen.

Carol/Hymn/Song – *suggestion*

Purify my heart

We will lay our burden down

Sing hey for the carpenter

PAYING ATTENTION TO OUR EMOTIONS

Reading – *Matthew 6.25–34*

'Therefore I tell you, do not worry about your life, what you will eat or what you will drink, or about your body, what you will wear. Is not life more than food, and the body more than clothing? Look at the birds of the air; they neither sow nor reap nor gather into barns, and yet your heavenly Father feeds them. Are you not of more value than they? And can any of you by worrying add a single hour to your span of life? And why do you worry about clothing? Consider the lilies of the field, how they grow; they neither toil nor spin, yet I tell you, even Solomon in all his glory was not clothed like one of these. But if God so clothes the grass of the field, which is alive today and tomorrow is thrown into the oven, will he not much more clothe you – you of little faith? Therefore, do not worry, saying, "What will we eat?" or "What will we drink?" or "What will we wear?" For it is the Gentiles who strive for all these things; and indeed your heavenly Father knows that you need all these things. But strive first for the kingdom of God and his righteousness, and all these things will be given to you as well. So do not worry about tomorrow, for tomorrow will bring worries of its own. Today's trouble is enough for today.'

Living Word of God,
speak within our hearts.

Reflection

Many people will carry a deep underlying sense of anxiety, a bag full of worries, with them. It's hard to see below the worries. One way of going deeper than the stresses and strains of everyday life is to pay attention to our feelings. The memories that we have focused on from the past year will have stirred a number of emotions: deep feelings of joy, excitement and pleasure, or of sadness, anger and fear. It is important for us to pay attention to our feelings, so that we are aware of them, noticing especially when we feel strongly, as this will often point to something that is going on beneath the surface. In the examen, as we focus on our feelings from the past year, or the past day, we stick with the two key questions:

- What has given me life?
- What has drained me?

Our feelings, our hearts, can help us choose what to embrace as life-giving, and what to avoid as life-diminishing. So we ask these two questions of ourselves, and offer to God all that surfaces for us:

- In the past year, what has given me life?
- And in the past year, what has drained me?

Cairn of Thanksgiving

A pile of stones can be a way of marking an important point on a journey, a landmark. This marker, this pile of stones, is called a 'cairn'. Together we are going to build a 'cairn of thanksgiving', a landmark acknowledging all our memories from the past year, both the joys and the sorrows.

As you place a stone for each significant memory, offer it with a prayer to God: 'I offer the whole of me, because you love the whole of me.'

Music is played as we build the cairn of thanksgiving.

Music – *suggestion*

Song for Athene – John Tavener

Prayers for Recognition

We bring to God our anxieties, our worries, our fears,
all that has clouded our hearts and minds,
and we let them go.
(Silence)

When the cares of my heart are many,
your consolations cheer my soul.
(Psalm 94.19)

We bring to God all that has drained us,
our anger, resentment and bitterness,
our guilt, shame and regret,
and we let them go.
(Silence)

When the cares of my heart are many,
your consolations cheer my soul.

We bring to God all the times we have been hurt,
our wounds, vulnerabilities and loss,
our arguments, disagreements and conflict,
and we let them go.
(Silence)

When the cares of my heart are many,
your consolations cheer my soul.

We bring to God all that has opened us to life,
our sense of connectedness, meaning and purpose,
our experience of beauty, wonder and deep peace,
and we offer them.
(Silence)

Seek first God's kingdom,
and all shall be given to you.

We bring to God all that has opened us to hope,
our imagination, our dreams and our creativity,
the gifts and abilities that have stretched our horizons,
and we offer them.
(Silence)

Seek first God's kingdom,
and all shall be given to you.

We bring to God all that has opened us to love,
whether from family, friends, home or community,
our sense of belonging, of being loved,
and we offer them.
(Silence)

Seek first God's kingdom,
and all shall be given to you.

Carol/Hymn/Song – *suggestions*

Through all the changing scenes of life

I heard the voice of Jesus say

In the bleak midwinter

Choosing and Praying from One Memory

Reading – *John 10.10*

I came to give life – life in all its fullness.

Reflection

We long to be fruitful, to grow, to thrive, to live. The person we will be in the future, who we will become, will depend on how we can choose the things that give us life and hope, and leave behind the things that damage and distort us. So we're going to take a moment to choose one particular memory that has been life-giving, and pray from that place, not just for ourselves, but for the world.

Shared Silence *(about five minutes)*

We choose one life-giving memory, and its positive emotions, as the place from which we pray, both for ourselves and for others, for our community and for our world.

LOOKING TOWARDS TOMORROW

New Year Response

So if anyone is in Christ,
there is a new creation:
everything old has passed away;
see, everything has become new!
(2 Corinthians 5.17)

Intercession

I will make a way in the wilderness
and rivers in the desert.
(Isaiah 43.19)

We pray for peace and reconciliation,
that the coming year may be a year of grace.
I will make a way in the wilderness
and rivers in the desert.

We pray for nurturing and growing, in our community
    and church,
that the coming year may be a year of grace.
I will make a way in the wilderness
and rivers in the desert.

We pray for creativity and plenty, in our working lives,
that the coming year may be a year of grace.
I will make a way in the wilderness
and rivers in the desert.

We pray for health and wholeness, for all who struggle,
that the coming year may be a year of grace.
I will make a way in the wilderness
and rivers in the desert.

We pray for resurrection life, for all who face death,
that the coming year may be a year of grace.
I will make a way in the wilderness
and rivers in the desert.

We look to the coming year,
its fears and challenges,
its hopes and possibilities.
We open our hearts
to all that the year ahead will contain,
and from that place of openness,
we name one hope for the year in our hearts.
I will make a way in the wilderness
and rivers in the desert.

Reflection

We are people of the covenant. We live in the light of God's unconditional love for us, knowing that there is nothing we can do to make God love us any more, nothing we can do to make God love us any less than God does already. For the coming year we recommit ourselves to the covenant love of God.

Covenant Prayer

**I am a child of God, made in your image and likeness,
I am included in the heart of your love.
You know me completely,
my faults and my weaknesses,
my gifts and my strengths.
You call me to live in the fullness of your love,
abundantly, generously, inclusively.**

You call me to empty myself, to serve as Jesus served,
willingly, humbly, selflessly.
You call me to bear witness to your presence,
boldly, courageously, gently.
You are the potter,
I am the clay.
Shape me, reshape me,
give me purpose and meaning,
energy and vision,
open me up as a channel of your grace.
May your covenant be written on my heart.
May my life reflect your promises.
What is true in heaven,
may it be seen in me,
within the dance of the Trinity of Love,
Father, Son and Holy Spirit.
Amen.

Carol/Hymn/Song – *suggestions*

Sing of the Lord's goodness

Guide me, O Thou great Redeemer

Thy hand, O God, has guided

Blessing

God of time and eternity,
alpha and omega,
beginning and end,
our future and our hope,
bless us now,
in your unconditional love,
that this may be a year of grace,
for us and for all humanity.
Amen.

EPIPHANY

Returning by Another Road

A celebration of difference, diversity and dialogue in a complex world

Introduction

You will need to provide all those attending with a paper star and a drawing pin. In a central position you will also need a map, on which people will pin their stars, showing where they come from. Have enough candles on a suitable stand for each person to come forward and light one.

Welcome

How are we to relate to people around us who come from many different nations, cultures and religions? It feels a very pressing question for us today, but it has been there from the earliest times. The visit of the Magi gives a pattern to us, helping us to relate to people who are different from us; it stretches our understanding of how God is revealed in a diverse world, connecting with us across differences.

Hymn/Song/Chant – *suggestions*

We three kings of Orient are

As with gladness

The splendour of the King

Opening Prayer

Unfamiliar God,
you come to us in strangers.
You are revealed through difference,
you stretch our imagination,
you provoke our questions.
Confound our comfortable certainties,
challenge our familiar ways of thinking,
call us to discover your unimagined depths,
as we journey together,
unexpected fellow travellers,
surprising companions,
pilgrims on the way,
following your star,
to love's fulfilment.
Amen.

Where do you come from?

Reading – *Matthew 2.1–2*

In the time of King Herod, after Jesus was born in Bethlehem
of Judea, wise men from the East came to Jerusalem, asking,
'Where is the child who has been born king of the Jews? For
we observed his star at its rising, and have come to pay him
homage.'

Reflection

Where do you come from? Were you born here? We are suspicious
of strangers, incomers, people of another culture, language or
colour. There are deep natural connections between people who
have come from a similar background; we like to be with people
who are like us, who think like us, who share a common outlook.
But there are dangers in tribalism! There is a laziness in choosing
to live in a ghetto! We don't have to think, we are not challenged

and we can become entrenched. Like Herod, we can then feel
threatened by change! The Magi crossed barriers not only of
distance but also of language, culture and religion – all in their
search for truth. They reached out, they questioned, they grew in
their faith and understanding. If we are to grow, we need to be
willing to travel beyond our known horizons, beyond our comfort zone, to set aside some of our prejudices and assumptions, to
open ourselves to new perspectives.

Prayers of Recognition

Unimaginable God,
we have made you too small,
we have tried to box you in to our own tradition,
to contain you in our own understanding.
We have made you in our own image,
when you long for us to grow in yours.
Help us now to see our prejudices, and to let them go.
(Silence)

In the company of strangers,
lead us as pilgrims on the way.

Ineffable God,
we have tried to constrain you,
through our doctrines and dogmas,
our churches and certainties,
to make you safe, manageable, predictable.
Help us now to recognize where we have become closed.
(Silence)

In the company of strangers,
lead us as pilgrims on the way.

Unexpected God,
you come to us in strangers,
like the Magi,
travellers, refugees, immigrants,

people of different faiths,
people of other traditions.
Help us to ask questions,
to listen, openly,
to welcome, with respect,
to share, generously,
that together, we may grow in you.
(Silence)

In the company of strangers,
lead us as pilgrims on the way.

ONE OF US?

Solidarity and affirmation of our common humanity

Music – *suggestion*

Le Onde – Ludovico Einaudi

You are invited to come and pin your star to the map to show where you come from, as a sign of our affirmation of our different paths to this place

Hymn/Song/Chant – *suggestions*

Brightest and best of the sons of the morning

O worship the Lord in the beauty of holiness

Laudate omnes gentes (Taizé)

WHO ARE YOU?

Reading – *Matthew 2.3–6*

When King Herod heard this, he was frightened, and all Jerusalem with him; and calling together all the chief priests and scribes of the people, he inquired of them where the Messiah was to be born. They told him, 'In Bethlehem of Judea; for so it has been written by the prophet:

"And you, Bethlehem, in the land of Judah,
are by no means least among the rulers of Judah;
for from you shall come a ruler
who is to shepherd my people Israel."'

Reflection

If we are to be open to other voices and other insights, that does not mean that we should be unsure of who we are, of our gospel, our values, our own faith. Some try to 'mix and match', choosing what they fancy from the different world religions. But true wisdom and true dialogue can only come when we are true to our own story. The Magi came to Herod to ask the way, to listen to the insights of the Jewish tradition. The priests and scribes went back to the prophets, to their scriptures, to the heart of their faith, to discover what might be meant. So we take time to value our own identity and story.

Prayer of Recognition

God of Abraham, of Isaac and of Jacob!
God of Ruth, of Esther, and of Mary!

We trace our story through so many lives,
rooted and grounded in your Love,
guided and taught through your Word,
nurtured and grown by your Spirit.
Holy God, holy and loving, holy and forgiving,
be our centre, our vision, our path.

Creator, Father, Abba,
Ruarch,* Mother, Wisdom,
we find our identity through your parenting,
known intimately, freed to become ourselves,
loved unconditionally, freed to choose our way,
held closely, freed to let go.
Holy God, holy and loving, holy and forgiving,
be our centre, our vision, our path.

Jesus, you invite us into a new identity in you,
as children of God through faith,
where there is neither Jew nor Greek,
neither slave nor free,
neither male nor female,
for we are all one in you.
Holy God, holy and loving, holy and forgiving,
be our centre, our vision, our path.

Shared Silence *(about five minutes)*

We think of all those who have taught us about God, inspired us in our walk of faith, and been an example for us to follow. We each come forward to light a candle to represent the light they have been for us.

Music may be played or a chant sung as the candles are lit

Chant – *suggestion*

The Lord is my light (Taizé)

---

* Hebrew: feminine for Spirit.

WHAT ARE YOU SAYING?

Reading - *Matthew 2.7-8*

Then Herod secretly called for the wise men and learned from them the exact time when the star had appeared. Then he sent them to Bethlehem, saying, 'Go and search diligently for the child; and when you have found him, bring me word so that I may also go and pay him homage.'

Reflection

There is a huge gap between Herod's words and his thoughts and intentions. He pretends that he wants to honour the child, while he is planning to kill him. We too have to 'mind the gap' between our faith and our lives. Jesus saved his greatest condemnation for hypocrites. It's so destructive to say one thing and do another: we have to 'walk the talk'. We are called to be salt of the earth, light of the world.

Prayer of Recognition

God of integrity,
you call us to be whole,
with hearts undivided,
with our lives reflecting our faith.
Give us grace to mirror your loving kindness.
(Silence)

Let us be salt of the earth,
light of the world.

Jesus, you showed us a life of love in action.
You call us to follow you,
for our lives to speak volumes.
Give us grace to be true disciples.
(Silence)

Let us be salt of the earth,
light of the world.

Spirit of truth, you live in us now.
You awaken in us an inner compass,
to guide and direct our path.
Give us grace to follow your heart.
(Silence)

Let us be salt of the earth,
light of the world.

Prayers of Intercession

We think of situations where the world desperately needs
integrity, honesty, and faith that is sincere.
For [*Name*],
Hear our prayer.
Touch our hearts.

We pray for places where there is
endemic corruption, oppression, prejudice, hatred.
For [*Name*],
Hear our prayer.
Touch our hearts.

We pray for places where religions have been distorted
to support terror, greed and poverty.
For [*Name*],
Hear our prayer.
Touch our hearts.

We pray for people of faith and integrity
to have courage to be salt and light in our world.
For [Name],
hear our prayer.
Touch our hearts.

Hymn/Song/Chant – *suggestions*

Father, hear the prayer we offer

Jesus, be the centre

O Lord, hear my prayer (Taizé)

WHAT ARE YOU HERE FOR?

Reading – *Matthew 2.9–11*

When they had heard the king, they set out; and there, ahead of them, went the star that they had seen at its rising, until it stopped over the place where the child was. When they saw that the star had stopped, they were overwhelmed with joy. On entering the house, they saw the child with Mary his mother; and they knelt down and paid him homage. Then, opening their treasure-chests, they offered him gifts of gold, frankincense, and myrrh.

Reflection

What are you here for? What is your real purpose in life? The Magi were here to visit the new-born child who was to change the world. They were here to kneel and worship, to give gifts. In a way, the visit to Herod was a distraction; it was not where Jesus was to be found. As Christians, perhaps particularly as the Church, we can get caught up in the daily grind of running an organization, and lose sight of our real purpose. We get distracted and deflected easily, and need to keep centring, returning to the heart of things, remembering our unique gifts, coming back to what we are really here for.

Prayer of Recognition

We use St Paul's letter to the Romans to remind us of our true calling and purpose (Romans 12.9–18).

Let love be genuine; hate what is evil,
hold fast to what is good;
love one another with mutual affection;
outdo one another in showing honour.
Give us the needful gifts of grace!

Do not lag in zeal, be ardent in spirit,
serve the Lord.
Rejoice in hope, be patient in suffering,
persevere in prayer.
Give us the needful gifts of grace!

Contribute to the needs of the saints;
extend hospitality to strangers.
Bless those who persecute you;
bless and do not curse them.
Rejoice with those who rejoice,
weep with those who weep.
Give us the needful gifts of grace!

Live in harmony with one another;
do not be haughty,
but associate with the lowly;
do not claim to be wiser than you are.
Give us the needful gifts of grace!

Do not repay anyone evil for evil,
but take thought for what is noble in the sight of all.
If it is possible, so far as it depends on you,
live peaceably with all.
Give us the needful gifts of grace!

May the God of all grace,
give to us all that is needful
to keep us true to our calling,
fixed to our purpose,
sure in our service,
that with the Magi
we may offer our unique gifts,
in the service of your love.
Amen.

Hymn/Song/Chant – *suggestions*

Who would think that what was needed

I will offer up my life

The Lord's my shepherd (Townend)

WHERE DO WE GO FROM HERE?

Reading – *Matthew 2.12*

And having been warned in a dream not to return to Herod, they left for their own country by another road.

Reflection

In any real encounter with God, we are changed. Our life takes a new direction: like the Magi, we return by another road. When life goes wrong it is easy to be tempted towards recrimination. Why has this happened to me? What have I done to deserve this? Who is to blame? But the only real question for people of faith is 'Where do we go from here?' So we ask God where our next steps will take us.

Prayer of Recognition

God of our next step,
you are always ahead of us,
drawing us further into your life and love,
stretching our capacity,
to walk with you.
(Silence)

Your word is a lamp to my feet,
and a light to my path.
(Psalm 119.105)

God of our next step,
you are always beside us,
opening new possibilities as we grow,
extending our vision,
to walk with you.
(Silence)

Your word is a lamp to my feet,
and a light to my path.

God of our next step,
you are always behind us,
encouraging us to move forward,
steadying our confidence,
to walk with you.
(Silence)

Your word is a lamp to my feet,
and a light to my path.

Blessing

God of the stranger,
bless us in our differences.
God of our true self,
bless us in our becoming.
God of integrity,
bless us in our true purpose.
God of our next step,
bless us in our daring to walk with you.
Father, Son, Spirit,
bless us with your needful gifts of grace.
Amen.

Hymn/Song/Chant – *suggestions*

Angels from the realms of glory

Angel voices, ever singing

Abundance

A celebration of God's overflowing grace, like water into wine

Introduction

Each of these sections would work as part of a regular service, perhaps as the Ministry of the Word at a Eucharist; or they could be used as one service, or as elements in a quiet day. You will need to provide three items for each person attending: a rock, an image of a hand, and a golden ribbon with safety pin.

Hymn/Song/Chant – *suggestions*

Come down, O Love divine

Teach me to dance

Confitemini Domino (Taizé)

Introduction

At some time in our lives most of us will experience insecurity. Nagging questions and fears about our place in the world are rooted in a deep-seated uncertainty. Are we really loved? Anxiety about food and drink almost always points to this deeper insecurity. In every encounter with people Jesus would go to the heart of this fear by including people in meals, and feeding the multitudes. As we explore this theme together we will ask some key questions underlying our security: Am I needed? Will there be enough for me? Have I missed out?

Opening Prayer

God in our uncertainty,
God in our doubts,
God in our deepest insecurity,
speak to us your word of peace;
show us our true worth in your eyes;
hold us in your unconditional love;
through Jesus, your living bread,
given for us, and for all.
Amen.

AM I NEEDED?

Reading – *John 2.1–5*

On the third day there was a wedding in Cana of Galilee, and the mother of Jesus was there. Jesus and his disciples had also been invited to the wedding. When the wine gave out, the mother of Jesus said to him, 'They have no wine.' And Jesus said to her, 'Woman, what concern is that to you and to me? My hour has not yet come.' His mother said to the servants, 'Do whatever he tells you.'

Reflection

We all long to be needed, to have a purpose, to be able to offer something. We don't want to feel useless, or to be a burden. Times of unemployment or failing health or disability can leave us asking, 'Am I needed?' At the heart of the Christian gospel is a promise that God's love for us is not dependent on our works or actions; it goes deeper than that, it is pure grace. At the wedding in Cana Mary sees the need, and Jesus seems to respond strangely, 'Woman, what concern is that to you and to me?' It's not a rebuke, but a reminder of a proper sense of detachment. Jesus at that moment doesn't need to be needed. He is living out of the deep security that comes from knowing that he is loved by God. When we find ourselves asking, 'Am I needed?', we need to return to the deeper question, 'Am I loved?' In that moment God says to us, 'You are my child, my beloved.' We are given rock-solid security that goes deeper than any unsteadiness.

Shared Silence *(about three minutes)*

We think of the times we have felt uncertain, insecure, full of doubt. We take hold of the rock we have chosen.

Responsive Psalm – *Psalm 61.1–4*

Hear my cry, O God;
listen to my prayer.
From the end of the earth I call to you,
when my heart is faint.
Lead me to the rock
that is higher than I;
for you are my refuge,
a strong tower against the enemy.
Let me abide in your tent for ever,
find refuge under the shelter of your wings.
Glory to the Father and to the Son and to the Holy Spirit.
As it was in the beginning, is now and shall be for ever. Amen.

Prayers for Recognition

We bring to God the moments of insecurity in our lives,
times of feeling useless or dependent,
not knowing if we are needed,
and we hold them in the stream of God's grace.
(Silence)

Set me on a rock
that is higher than I.

We bring to God the moments of uncertainty in our lives,
unsure of our relationships,
when love seems scarce or jaded,
and we hold them in the stream of God's grace.
(Silence)

Set me on a rock
that is higher than I.

We bring to God the moments of self-doubt in our lives,
unsure of our own worth,
even in our faith,
and we hold them in the stream of God's grace.
(Silence)

Set me on a rock
that is higher than I.

Intercession

For all who feel unneeded, left behind, or unwanted,
through ageing, unemployment, or the breakdown of
    relationships.
Hear my cry, O God;
listen to my prayer.

For all who feel insecure or unsafe, or vulnerable,
through fleeing conflict, homelessness, the fear of crime,
    or abuse.
Hear my cry, O God;
listen to my prayer.

For all who feel useless, powerless, or isolated,
through illness or disability, mental health, or loneliness.
Hear my cry, O God;
listen to my prayer.

Prayer

Rock of ages,
ground of our being,
foundation of our becoming,
bedrock of our living,
support us as we grow,
steady us when we are shaken,
so that we may flourish,
in the deep security of your love
revealed in Jesus.
Amen.

You are invited to keep and carry the rock you have chosen to be a daily reminder of God's deep love for you, and your deep security in God's holding love.

Hymn/Song/Chant – *suggestions*

Rock of ages

In Christ alone

Stand, O stand firm (Wild Goose Worship)

WILL THERE BE ENOUGH FOR ME?

Reading – *John 2.6–8*

Now standing there were six stone water-jars for the Jewish rites of purification, each holding 20 or 30 gallons. Jesus said to them, 'Fill the jars with water.' And they filled them up to the brim. He said to them, 'Now draw some out, and take it to the chief steward.' So they took it.

Reflection

It seems an extraordinary amount of wine, more than could possibly have been needed. What a party! The image of a wedding feast is a familiar picture of the coming kingdom of God, and this account wants us to be in no doubt that there will be enough wine, enough of God's love, for everyone. In the other feeding miracles, of the multitudes, when Jesus took the seemingly inadequate offering of bread and fish, once more there was enough, more than enough, with basketfuls left over. When we are anxious about food – will there be enough for me? – we are anxious about whether we are loved. As we open our hands, God says to us, 'I am the bread of life, come to me and never be hungry.'

Shared Silence *(about three minutes)*

We think of the times we have asked: 'Will there be enough for me?' We take hold of the image of a hand we have chosen.

Responsive Psalm – *Psalm 145.13–16*

The Lord is faithful in all his words,
and gracious in all his deeds.
The Lord upholds all who are falling,
and raises up all who are bowed down.
The eyes of all look to you,
and you give them their food in due season.
You open your hand,
satisfying the desire of every living thing.
Glory to the Father and to the Son and to the Holy Spirit.
As it was in the beginning, is now and shall be for ever.
Amen.

Prayers of Recognition

People may like to sit with open hands for these prayers

We bring to God the times we have felt inadequate,
when we have run out of energy, or time,
when we have exhausted our patience, or compassion,
when we have lost our perspective on something.
With empty hands we are open to God's grace.
(Silence)

You open your hand,
satisfying the desire of every living thing.

We bring to God our complex relationship with eating
    and drinking,
our fears that there won't be enough for us,
our consuming too much or too little.
With empty hands we are open to God's grace.
(Silence)

You open your hand,
satisfying the desire of every living thing.

We bring to God our fragile faith,
our doubts and uncertainties,
our fears that we are not good enough,
that we don't know enough.
With empty hands we are open to God's grace.
(Silence)

You open your hand,
satisfying the desire of every living thing.

Intercession

For all who are 'running on empty', drained, and feeling
   inadequate,
through carrying too much responsibility.
The Lord upholds all who are falling,
and raises up all who are bowed down.

For all who are struggling with their health,
through chronic fatigue, dementia, or terminal illness.
The Lord upholds all who are falling,
and raises up all who are bowed down.

For all who are carers, unsupported or overstretched,
through cutbacks in care, inadequate services, or isolation.
The Lord upholds all who are falling,
and raises up all who are bowed down.

Prayer

Open-handed God,
generous giver of grace,
abundant source of life,
fill us with your nourishing goodness,
satisfy our deepest hunger,
and strengthen us to reach out to others
in the deep security of your love,
revealed in Jesus.
Amen.

*You are invited to keep and carry the hand you have chosen to
be a daily reminder of God's abundant love for you and for the
world, and of our deep security in God's hand.*

Hymn/Song/Chant – *suggestions*

Guide me, O Thou great Redeemer

Give thanks with a grateful heart

Glory and gratitude and praise (Wild Goose Worship)

HAVE I MISSED OUT?

Reading – *John 2.9–11*

When the steward tasted the water that had become wine, and did not know where it came from (though the servants who had drawn the water knew), the steward called the bridegroom and said to him, 'Everyone serves the good wine first, and then the inferior wine after the guests have become drunk. But you have kept the good wine until now.' Jesus did this, the first of his signs, in Cana of Galilee, and revealed his glory; and his disciples believed in him.

Reflection

There is a gritty, wry honesty to this account of the steward's response when tasting the water made into wine. Everyone knows that we are careful of the best wine, the best things in life; we don't want them to be wasted. Many people live their lives with a lingering anxiety that they have 'missed out'. We are sometimes envious of the lives that others seem to live, their cars, houses, holidays, and feel that the 'grass is always greener on the other side of the fence'. Or we look back to a 'golden age' when life was so much better. Have I missed out? But here, the steward is surprised – 'You have saved the best wine till now!' In the very place where we think we are running out, we find Jesus, the best wine of all.

Shared Silence *(about three minutes)*

We think of the times we have asked: 'Have I missed out?' We take hold of the golden ribbon and safety pin we have chosen.

Responsive Psalm – *Psalm 104.1–2, 13–15*

Bless the Lord, O my soul.
O Lord my God, you are very great.
You are clothed with honour and majesty,
wrapped in light as with a garment.
You stretch out the heavens like a tent.
From your lofty abode you water the mountains;
the earth is satisfied with the fruit of your work.
You cause the grass to grow for the cattle,
and plants for people to use,
to bring forth food from the earth,
and wine to gladden the human heart,
oil to make the face shine,
and bread to strengthen the human heart.
Glory to the Father and to the Son and to the Holy Spirit.
As it was in the beginning, is now and shall be for ever.
Amen.

Prayers of Recognition

We bring to God the times when we feel we have missed out,
our memories of hardships, of lost opportunities, and regrets.
We bring them to the abundance of God's love.
(Silence)

The best wine
you have saved until now!

We bring to God the times we have felt let down by the
    present day,
our sense of the 'good old days', of better times past, of sadness.
We bring them to the abundance of God's love.
(Silence)

The best wine
you have saved until now!

We bring to God the times we have felt envious and resentful,
of others' good fortune, achievements, or recognition.
We bring them to the abundance of God's love.
(Silence)

The best wine
you have saved until now!

Intercession

For all who are overlooked and ignored,
for the poor, marginalized and oppressed,
whose voices have not been heard.
(Silence)

You give oil to make the face shine,
bread to strengthen the human heart.

For all who are undervalued,
for those on low wages, in low-status jobs.
(Silence)

You give oil to make the face shine,
bread to strengthen the human heart.

For all who long for change, but can see none.
(Silence)

You give oil to make the face shine,
bread to strengthen the human heart.

Blessing

Rock of ages, steady us.
Hand of grace, feed us.
Golden thread, enlighten us
to see that you've saved the best till now.
Bless us with your abundance,
Father, Son and Spirit,
Trinity of Love.
Amen.

Hymn/Song/Chant – *suggestions*

Fill your hearts with joy and gladness

Blessed be your name

Sing of the Lord's goodness

Becoming Good News

A blessing for our community

Introduction

There are three movements in this service, and you will need to create a space to bring these together. People come forward to make a spiral of stones, and later bring their written responses to lay around the stones, then they light a candle beside their responses. So you will need: small stones (polished ones can be sourced from a garden centre); paper and pens; a supply of tea lights or votive candles. For large numbers of people you may want to reduce the number of movements they make as it can add greatly to the time. You will also need some olive oil for anointing.

Welcome

If our church was closed down, who would miss us? How far have we become turned in on ourselves, preoccupied with our own institutions? Is our church a blessing to the people of our wider community? As we look again at the very beginning of Jesus' public teaching, we ask how we can become more like the good news that Jesus announced.

Hymn/Song/Chant – *suggestions*

God's Spirit is in my heart

Restore, O Lord, the honour

Mayenziwe (Wild Goose Worship)

Prayer

God, who so loves the world
that you sent your Son,
give us grace to love like him,
to become channels
of your good news to all people,
in Jesus' name.
Amen.

CUSTOM

Reading – *Luke 4.16–21*

When he came to Nazareth, where he had been brought up, he went to the synagogue on the Sabbath day, as was his custom. He stood up to read, and the scroll of the prophet Isaiah was given to him. He unrolled the scroll and found the place where it was written:

'The Spirit of the Lord is upon me,
because he has anointed me
to bring good news to the poor.
He has sent me to proclaim release to the captives
and recovery of sight to the blind,
to let the oppressed go free,
to proclaim the year of the Lord's favour.'

And he rolled up the scroll, gave it back to the attendant, and sat down. The eyes of all in the synagogue were fixed on him. Then he began to say to them, 'Today this scripture has been fulfilled in your hearing.'

Living Word of God,
speak within our hearts.

Reflection

We begin on familiar territory: Jesus came to his home town of Nazareth, returning to his home synagogue, for the usual service on the Sabbath, as was his custom. There can be great strength in familiarity and custom: we love the certainty of the known way.

Prayers of Recognition

We think of our own customs of faith and worship, and of what is familiar to us. We give thanks for all that sustains us in our faith and gives us life.

Shared Silence *(about three minutes)*

Thanksgiving

God of our earliest memory,
we give you thanks for happy memories
from childhood and times past,
blessings of home, family and old friends,
for our sense of place and belonging.

Where you go, I will go;
where you lodge, I will lodge;
your people shall be my people,
and your God my God.
(Ruth 1.16)

We give you thanks for faith's awakening,
ears opening to your Word,
eyes opening to your presence,
mind shaping to your call,
heart warming to your love,
for our sense of meaning and purpose.

Where you go, I will go;
where you lodge, I will lodge;
your people shall be my people,
and your God my God.

We give you thanks for faith's maturing,
struggling with life and experience,
wrestling with certainty and questions,
grappling with love and difference,
for our sense of deepening and broadening.

Where you go, I will go;
where you lodge, I will lodge;
your people shall be my people,
and your God my God.

Song/Chant – *suggestions*

Jesus, be the centre

Take, O take me as I am (Wild Goose Worship)

Abba Father

During the singing we will create a spiral of pebbles to represent the growing and nurturing of our faith, as individuals and as a church.

We come forward to place a pebble.

Reflection

Custom and tradition have their strengths, but custom and tradition can also become stultifying, a rut that can too easily become a grave! We can find ourselves going through the motions of faith, but losing the connection with God. Custom can also allow us to become disconnected from those around us, especially in changing times. Rituals and traditions that have been life-giving to us can seem distant or excluding to others who have not shared the story that has shaped those traditions. When sharing with people who have not been brought up in a tradition of Christian faith, we need to notice whether our worship is connecting with their experience, their deep spiritual needs.

Prayers of Recognition

We bring to God the ways in which our church has
    turned inwards,
times when we are anxious about declining congregations,
times when we are preoccupied by financial difficulties,
times when we spend our energies keeping 'the show on
    the road'.
(Silence)

O sing to the Lord a new song;
sing to the Lord, all the earth.
(Psalm 96.1)

We bring to God the ways in which our church has got stuck in
    the past,
times when we have chosen the conventional or respectable path,
times when we have preferred the comfort of the familiar ways,
times when we have missed the challenge of the new.
(Silence)

O sing to the Lord a new song;
sing to the Lord, all the earth.

We bring to God the ways in which our faith has become stale,
times when we have been closed to new ideas and possibilities,
times when we have been deaf to your call to change,
times when we have failed to see you in our neighbour.
(Silence)

O sing to the Lord a new song;
sing to the Lord, all the earth.

Words of Assurance

Do not remember the former things,
nor consider the things of old.
I am about to do a new thing;
now it springs forth, do you not perceive it?
(Isaiah 43.18–19)

God, you are the same, yesterday, today and for ever!
You are the rock, the foundation on which we build
  with confidence,
you are the constant presence in our living,
you are the energy in our growing.
Give us confidence,
to let go of the old ways that have become stale.
Give us vision,
to see the new thing that you are doing.
Give us energy,
to embrace the possibilities of tomorrow,
in Jesus who fills and fulfils us.
Amen.

Hymn/Song/Chant – *suggestions*

Be thou my vision

Yesterday, today and forever

Behold, I make all things new (Wild Goose Worship)

CHANGE

Reflection

Jesus came to reconnect people with God. Like John the Baptist, he called us to repent, to be willing to change our minds, to see things with fresh eyes, to have a completely new outlook. He was handed the scroll of the prophet Isaiah, and chose to read:

> The Spirit of the Lord is upon me,
> because he has anointed me
> to bring good news to the poor.
> He has sent me to proclaim release to the captives
> and recovery of sight to the blind,
> to let the oppressed go free,
> to proclaim the year of the Lord's favour.
> (Isaiah 61.1–2)

Instead of being turned in on ourselves, this is a call to turn outwards. Instead of being preoccupied with our own concerns, Jesus points us to look outwards to others who may be unconnected with faith or the institution of the church, who may not be remembered or respectable. Can we follow Jesus in bringing good news to the poor, release to captives, sight for the blind, freedom for the oppressed? If this is our aim, what does our shared life in Christ look like? How can our church be a blessing to our local community? What needs to change?

Shared Silence *(about three minutes)*

We spend a few minutes in silence, thinking about these questions

How can our church be a blessing to our local community?

What needs to change?

Make a note of the ideas that come to you as a way of listening to your own heart and being open to the prompting of God's Holy Spirit

Then we turn to our neighbour and discuss our response

Prayer

Lord Jesus,
you call us to be,
not just to preach,
or to pray,
but to be:
good news to the poor,
release for the captives,
sight for the blind,
freedom for the oppressed;
and by this,
to proclaim your favour.
We ask you to help us,
to turn our hearts inside out,
to turn our world upside down,
to turn us to proclaim
the eternal jubilee of your love
in all we do and say.
Amen.

Music is played as we place our papers around the spiral of stones

Beside each one, light a candle, offering our response to God and to one another

Music – *suggestion*

A Gaelic Blessing – John Rutter

Prayers of Intercession

Jesus, we pray for all who struggle with poverty,
through low income, debt or conflict,
in our local community and in the wider world.
Help us to overcome the poverty of our own response.
May we know the good news of your love.
Your kingdom come,
your will be done.

Jesus, we pray for all who are held captive,
through infirmity or addiction, fear or imprisonment.
Help us to find release from the captivity of our own inaction.
May we all know release from all that binds.
Your kingdom come,
your will be done.

Jesus, we pray for all who are blind,
through disability, prejudice or ignorance.
Open our eyes where we have lost sight of your world.
May we all recover our vision.
Your kingdom come,
your will be done.

Jesus, we pray for all who are oppressed,
through cruelty, bullying or injustice.
Break down the bars of our apathy.
May we all be set free.
Your kingdom come,
your will be done.

Our Father, who art in heaven,
hallowed be thy name;
thy kingdom come,
thy will be done;
on earth as it is in heaven.
Give us this day our daily bread.
And forgive us our trespasses,
as we forgive those who trespass against us.
And lead us not into temptation;
but deliver us from evil.
For thine is the kingdom, the power, and the glory,
for ever and ever.
Amen.

Hymn/Song/Chant – *suggestions*

Make me a channel of your peace

Christ's the world in which we move

Ubi caritas (Taizé)

BECOMING A BLESSING

Reflection

Breaking through all custom and expectation, Jesus makes an extraordinary claim as he finishes reading.

> And he rolled up the scroll, gave it back to the attendant, and sat down. The eyes of all in the synagogue were fixed on him. Then he began to say to them, 'Today this scripture has been fulfilled in your hearing.' (Luke 4.20–21)

The single word 'today' has an explosive power to it! God is acting not in some far-off future, not in the distant past, but now, today, to fulfil this prophecy. It holds the same power for us. Today, now, God is asking us to become part of the good news, to become part of loving, freeing, healing the world, to join in! We are called to be a blessing to our local community and the global community.

Becoming a Blessing

Enable us to live our lives faithfully,
forgiving others when they hurt us,
turning the other cheek.
(Silence)

Today, you call us to be a blessing.
Fulfil in us your promises.

Enable us to see your image in other people,
accepting people who are different,
welcoming the stranger.
(Silence)

Today, you call us to be a blessing.
Fulfil in us your promises.

Enable us to weep with those who are sorrowful
and laugh with those who are joyful,
living in harmony with all.
(Silence)

Today, you call us to be a blessing.
Fulfil in us your promises.

Enable us to stand with those who are in need,
honouring their unique gifts,
working for justice for all.
(Silence)

Today, you call us to be a blessing.
Fulfil in us your promises.

Prayer

God of all blessing,
you call us to live fully,
to love generously,
and to become part of your good news.
May we, and our churches,
turn out from ourselves,
reaching out in your love,
sharing the treasures of your abundance,
in Jesus' name.
Amen.

Anointing

We come forward to receive anointing with oil to affirm our commitment to become people of good news, a blessing to our community.

Music is played

Music – *suggestion*

The Armed Man: Benedictus – Karl Jenkins

A member of the congregation anoints the minister's hands, making the sign of the cross on each open palm, saying:
Live fully, love generously, become blessing!

The minister then anoints the people, in the same way, saying:
Live fully, love generously, become blessing!

Closing Responses

If then there is any encouragement in Christ,
any consolation from love,
any sharing in the Spirit,
any compassion and sympathy,
make my joy complete:
be of the same mind,
having the same love,
being in full accord and of one mind.
Do nothing from selfish ambition or conceit,
but in humility regard others as better than yourselves.
Let each of you look not to your own interests,
but to the interests of others.
(Philippians 2.1–4)

Blessing

Spirit of God,
poured out for all your children,
fill our hearts and minds
with your encouragement and consolation,
your compassion and sympathy.
Make us one,
to be good news in our community,
to be blessing in your world,
in Jesus
who fulfils your promise
in us today.
Amen.

Hymn/Song/Chant – *suggestions*

Go forth and tell

Heaven shall not wait

Days of Elijah

Candlemas – Presentation of Christ in the Temple

Comfort and challenge in our darkness

Introduction

This service is designed to give some of the atmosphere of worship from the Taizé Community; it takes up the Candlemas themes of darkness and light. It is an opportunity to create a space that can be very different from a usual Sunday service. You might choose to use an open part of the church and form a circle; or you could ask people to sit opposite one another. If possible the lights should be lowered, and the space lit and defined by candlelight. People should gather in subdued lighting, and receive an unlit candle as they arrive. You could sing chants as people gather, or to use this time to teach the chants. A rough wooden cross needs to be placed in the centre or at one end of the space. Set out enough tea lights closely around the cross for everyone to be able to light one during the service.

Gathering Chant – *suggestion*

The kingdom of God is justice and peace (Taizé)

Opening Prayer

Child of our longing,
hope of ancient days,
comfort for the lowly,
challenge for the proud,
you come to challenge our established structures of power,
you come for the falling and rising of many.
Come now and open our hearts
to your presence in our midst.
Amen.

Prayers of Recognition

Mary and Joseph brought the sacrifice of the poor,
a pair of turtle doves,
all they could afford,
to give thanks for the birth of their son.
Lord Jesus, what shall we bring?
(Silence)

We come with empty hands.
Fill us with your grace.

Simeon and Anna waited patiently in the Temple,
hoping and longing
for God's promises to be fulfilled.
Lord Jesus, what shall we hope for?
(Silence)

We come with empty hands.
Fill us with your grace.

We come to this place, to this moment,
offering all that we are,
all that we have,
all that we hope to become.
Lord Jesus, we come to you.
(Silence)

We come with empty hands.
Fill us with your grace.

Prayers of Confession

The Lord whom you seek
will suddenly come to his temple.
The messenger of the covenant in whom you delight,
indeed, he is coming, says the Lord of hosts.
But who can endure the day of his coming,
and who can stand when he appears?
For he is like a refiner's fire and like fullers' soap;
he will sit as a refiner and purifier of silver.
(Malachi 3.1–3)

Shared Silence *(about three minutes)*

We hold a time of silence as we remember how much God loves us

Chant – *suggestion*

    Kyrie, kyrie, kyrie eleison (Taizé)
    (We sing the chant after each prayer)

Prayer

Loving God, refining fire,
you know us through and through;
nothing is hidden from your gaze.
You look for the best in us,
you look beyond our faults and failings,
you look into our hearts.
(Silence)

Lord, have mercy on us.
Kyrie, kyrie, kyrie eleison.

Loving God, refining fire,
we hardly know ourselves;
we hide behind false images;
we can too easily look for
the worst in ourselves and in others,
failing to look below the surface.
(Silence)

Lord, have mercy on us.
Kyrie, kyrie, kyrie eleison.

Loving God, refining fire,
help us to see through your eyes,
like Simeon and Anna,
to see the opportunities you present,
the promises you fulfil,
to see the best in ourselves and in others,
and to live from that perception.
(Silence)

Lord, have mercy on us.
Kyrie, kyrie, kyrie eleison.

The Assurance of Forgiveness

God for us
in our becoming,
God with us
in our journeying,
God in us
in our healing.
God, Father, Son and Holy Spirit,
forgive us and make us whole.
Amen.

Responsive Psalm – *Psalm 67*

Let the peoples praise you, O God;
let all the peoples praise you.

May God be gracious to us and bless us,
and make his face to shine upon us.
that your way may be known upon earth,
your saving power among all nations.
Let the peoples praise you, O God;
let all the peoples praise you.

Let the nations be glad and sing for joy,
for you judge the peoples with equity
and guide all the nations upon earth.
Let the peoples praise you, O God;
let all the peoples praise you.

The earth has yielded its increase;
God, our God, has blessed us.
May God continue to bless us;
let all the ends of the earth revere him.
Let the peoples praise you, O God;
let all the peoples praise you.

Chant – *suggestion*

Jesus, your Spirit in us is a wellspring of life everlasting (Taizé)

Reading – *Luke 2.22–24*

When the time came for their purification according to the law
of Moses, Mary and Joseph brought Jesus up to Jerusalem to
present him to the Lord (as it is written in the law of the Lord,
'Every firstborn male shall be designated as holy to the Lord'),
and they offered a sacrifice according to what is stated in the law
of the Lord, 'a pair of turtle-doves or two young pigeons.'

Reflection

Mary and Joseph might have brought a lamb to give thanks for the birth of their first-born son, but they couldn't afford it, so they brought the sacrifice of the poor, two young pigeons. The slaughter of animals to appease an angry God seems a million miles away from our own experience today: sacrifice is a less familiar term for us. More often our culture speaks of self-fulfilment than of self-sacrifice. Where do we come across sacrifice today? We seem to sacrifice more and more of our lives to work, to earning enough to pay the bills, to maintaining our standard of living. We may be called on to sacrifice our freedom to care for elderly relatives, or a sick partner. We might make sacrifices to support the children, putting their needs first. And we remember those who made the supreme sacrifice, giving their lives in time of war. Above all, we are called to be people who live sacrificially by giving of ourselves, to be wholehearted in our relationships, to live for others in our community.

As Christians we are called to be 'living sacrifices', to live lives that are dedicated to God, to live in a sacrificial way, to live generously. Candlemas helps us to ask, 'How can I live sacrificially?' Let's keep a time of silence now to be with that question.

Silence *(about three minutes)*

We consider the question, 'How can I live sacrificially?'

Reading – *Luke 2.25–28*

> Now there was a man in Jerusalem whose name was Simeon; this man was righteous and devout, looking forward to the consolation of Israel, and the Holy Spirit rested on him. It had been revealed to him by the Holy Spirit that he would not see death before he had seen the Lord's Messiah. Guided by the Spirit, Simeon came into the temple; and when the parents brought in the child Jesus, to do for him what was customary under the law, Simeon took him in his arms and praised God, saying,

Now, Lord, you let your servant go in peace:
your word has been fulfilled.
My own eyes have seen the salvation
which you have prepared in the sight of every people;
A light to reveal you to the nations
and the glory of your people Israel.
(*Common Worship*)

Reading – *Luke 2.33–35*

And the child's father and mother were amazed at what was being said about him.

Then Simeon blessed them and said to his mother Mary, 'This child is destined for the falling and the rising of many in Israel, and to be a sign that will be opposed so that the inner thoughts of many will be revealed – and a sword will pierce your own soul too.'

Reflection

When Simeon said that this child Jesus would be a light to the nations, he knew that one person's light is another person's darkness, that good news for some will mean bad news for others. In Jesus' case, good news for the poor would mean bad news for the rich; good news for the vulnerable, the widow and orphan, the excluded and unclean, would mean bad news for the powerful. This child is destined for the falling and the rising of many in Israel, and to be a sign that will be opposed. In his life, Jesus turned things upside down; he raised up the lowly and cast down the mighty from their thrones, he scandalized the religious by daring to include the lost and the unloved. He dared to unlock the love of God from the Temple and to release it in the marketplace. He was far from comfortable: his life was like a sword that could pierce the soul. In our own lives, what needs changing? Where are we too comfortable?

Let's take some time in this next silence to ponder that question.

Silence *(about three minutes)*

We consider the question, 'In our own lives, what needs changing?'

Reading – *Luke 2.36–40*

There was also a prophet, Anna the daughter of Phanuel, of
the tribe of Asher. She was of a great age, having lived with her
husband seven years after her marriage, then as a widow to the
age of 84. She never left the temple but worshipped there with
fasting and prayer night and day. At that moment she came, and
began to praise God and to speak about the child to all who
were looking for the redemption of Jerusalem.

When they had finished everything required by the law of the
Lord, they returned to Galilee, to their own town of Nazareth.
The child grew and became strong, filled with wisdom; and the
favour of God was upon him.

Reflection

God sometimes speaks through unexpected people – and we can
be surprised by the people that God chooses. Anna was a widow,
just one of the old ladies who went to the Temple all the time. She
wasn't a priest, or an official person: she couldn't have been, as
at that time they didn't allow women even to enter the innermost
parts of the temple. She had had a hard life, widowed after only
seven years of marriage; and she was now near the end of her
life. The very old and the very young have so much in common.
Through the eyes of her wisdom and through the long years of
prayer and waiting on God, Anna could see the potential wrapped
up in the tiny helpless child. She could see the man he would
become, and the hope that he would bring to an unhappy world.
I wonder what it is that is wrapped up in your heart. What is it
that God has in store for you? It doesn't matter if we are very old
or very young, or somewhere in the middle – God does have a
core purpose for each and every one of us, and he longs for us to
discover it and to live into it.

So let's wait on God now with that question in this next silence.

Silence *(about three minutes)*

We consider the questions, 'What is it that God has in store for you? What is your core purpose?'

Prayers of Intercession

Chant – *suggestion*

Nothing can trouble (Taizé)
(We sing the chant after each prayer)

Child of the poor,
hope of the outcast,
delight of the unloved,
you come to us in helpless vulnerability.
Be with all those who feel helpless and vulnerable now.
Nothing can trouble ...

Child in the temple,
greeted by Simeon,
light of the nations,
you come to bring light to dark places.
Be with all who struggle in darkness now.
Nothing can trouble ...

Child of the people,
recognized by Anna,
bringing us freedom,
you come to those who long for freedom.
Be with all who are held in bondage now.
Nothing can trouble ...

Child of justice,
destined for the falling and rising of many,
you come to turn us upside down.
Be with all who long for justice now.
Nothing can trouble ...

Child of perception,
you come to reveal our inner thoughts,
to call us to yourself.
Be with all who have lost their way now.
Nothing can trouble ...

Child of opposition,
you come to call us to a different way,
to challenge the values of our world.
Be with us as we walk your way of transforming love.
Nothing can trouble ...

**Our Father, who art in heaven,
hallowed be thy name,
thy kingdom come,
thy will be done,
on earth as it is in heaven.
Give us this day our daily bread.
And forgive us our trespasses,
as we forgive those who trespass against us.
And lead us not into temptation,
but deliver us from evil.
For thine is the kingdom, the power, and the glory,
for ever and ever.
Amen.**

Candle Lighting

*Music is played as we come forward to light candles around
the cross to renew our commitment to shine as lights in the
darkness, and to ask God to shine through our living*

Music *– suggestion*

Nunc Dimittis – Arvo Pärt

Blessing

Bless to us your light in our darkness;
bless to us your hope in our hearts;
bless to us your peace in our homes.
And the blessing of God,
Father, Son and Holy Spirit,
be with us,
now and for ever.
Amen.

Final Chant – *suggestion*

In the Lord I'll be ever thankful (Taizé)

SAMPLE SERVICE SHEETS

The Child Who is to Come

Advent pilgrimage

A sample service sheet for the service on page 29.

A CELEBRATION OF ADVENT

Music

Welcome

Hymn

HOPING

Prayer

God of our deepest longing,
all our hopes are met in you.
You hear our heart's cry,
you know our deepest need.
Meet us in this place,
speak to us through the silence,
touch us with your healing love,
that we may share your hopes for the whole creation,
in and through Jesus, the child who is to come.
Amen.

VOICES OF HOPE

Reflection

We take a purple ribbon and hold it, letting it symbolize our
hopelessness – in the quietness we name in our hearts where we
feel hopeless, anxious, afraid.
(A few moments of silence)

We take a yellow ribbon and hold it, letting it symbolize for us
our hope – in the quietness we name in our hearts where we feel
hopeful, excited, alive.
(A few moments of silence)

As we sing the chant, we come forward to tie our ribbons to the
cross, offering the whole of ourselves to God.

Chant

Bless the Lord, my soul, and bless God's holy name.
Bless the Lord, my soul, God leads me into life. (Taizé)

Prayers of Recognition

We bring to God all that feels hopeless in us,
our disappointments, our regrets;
and hold them in the light of God's assurance,
for us and for all creation.
(Silence)

No one who hopes in you
will ever be put to shame.

We bring to God all that is hopeful in us,
our dreams and aspirations;
and hold them in the light of God's hopes
for us and all creation.
(Silence)

No one who hopes in you
will ever be put to shame.

Hope of the world, as you called Mary to share your hopes and
    dreams,
may we respond with her:
Let it be with me according to your word.

Hope of the hopeless, as you called Joseph
beyond his disappointment,
may we respond with him:
Let it be with me according to your word.

Hope of all the nations, as you look in sorrow
at what we have become,
may we all respond:

Let it be with me according to your word.
Amen.

Hymn

WAITING

Prayer

God of all time and eternity,
every moment of our lives is held in you.
You call us to be still and to wait with you.
Meet us in this place,
speak to us through the silence,
touch us with your healing love,
that we may rise up on eagles' wings,
in and through Jesus, the child who is to come.
Amen.

VOICES OF WAITING

Reflection

Chant

Wait for the Lord whose day is near,
wait for the Lord, keep watch, take heart. (Taizé)

Silence

'Be still and know that I am God.'

Chant

Wait for the Lord whose day is near,
wait for the Lord, keep watch, take heart. (Taizé)

Prayers of Recognition

We bring to God our busyness,
all that is frenetic, all that is jaded, all that is exhausted in us:
(Silence)

Wait for the Lord.
Keep watch, take heart.

We bring to God our impatience,
our frustrations and our unhappiness.
(Silence)

Wait for the Lord.
Keep watch, take heart.

We bring to God all that we are waiting for.
(Silence)

Wait for the Lord.
Keep watch, take heart.

> Be patient, therefore, beloved, until the coming of the Lord. The farmer waits for the precious crop from the earth, being patient with it until it receives the early and the late rains. (James 5.7)

Holy Spirit of God, we wait for you.
Speak to us in your still small voice of calm.
Renew our strength, restore our faith, refresh our vision.
Help us to wait for you through these weeks of Advent,
to make space,
to welcome the Word made flesh,
Jesus the child who is to come.
Amen.

Hymn

FEARING

Prayer

God of perfect love
you help us to face our fears,
to know the truth about ourselves,
to be set free to grow and change.
You call us not to be afraid.
Meet us in this place,
speak to us through the silence,
touch us with your healing love,
that we may know you,
in and through Jesus, the child who is to come.
Amen.

VOICES OF FEARING

Reflection

Prayers of Intercession

Don't be afraid, my love is stronger,
my love is stronger than your fears.
Don't be afraid, my love is stronger,
and I have promised, promised to be always near.
(Wild Goose Worship)

For all who are fearful for the future,
for mothers bringing children into a fearful world,
for refugees and those caught up in conflict.
Don't be afraid ...

For all who are fearful for their health,
of growing older, of losing independence,
for those who are becoming confused, those awaiting test results.
Don't be afraid ...

For all who are fearful in an uncertain world of work,
of unemployment or redundancy,
of how to make ends meet and pay the bills.
Don't be afraid ...

For all who are fearful in relationships,
or of being alone and uncared for,
for those who are unhappy and feeling trapped.
Don't be afraid ...

God of perfect love,
cast out the fears that overshadow our lives.
Light of love, push back the darkness that hems us in,
that we may walk with confidence,
even into an uncertain future,
even in a fearful world,
with and through the child who is to come, Christ Jesus.
Amen.

Our Father, who art in heaven,
hallowed be thy name;
thy kingdom come,
thy will be done,
on earth as it is in heaven.
Give us this day our daily bread.
And forgive us our trespasses,
as we forgive those who trespass against us.
And lead us not into temptation,
but deliver us from evil.
For thine is the kingdom, the power, and the glory,
for ever and ever.
Amen.

Hymn

PREPARING

Prayer

Gracious God,
you prepare a way in the wilderness,
a table for our sustenance,
good things for our journeying.
You call us to prepare a way in our hearts.
Meet us in this place,
speak to us through the silence,
touch us with your healing love,
that we may prepare our lives for change,
in and through Jesus, the child who is to come.
Amen.

VOICES PREPARING

Reflection

Wilderness Time

Chant

The kingdom of God is justice and peace
and joy in the Holy Spirit!
Come, Lord, and open in us
the gates of your kingdom! (Taizé)

Prayers of Recognition

We offer to God our commitment to change,
to be different from this moment,
to prepare our hearts to meet him.
Prepare the way of the Lord.
Make his paths straight.

We offer to God all that we would clear out,
simplify and leave behind,
to prepare our hearts to meet him.
Prepare the way of the Lord.
Make his paths straight.

We offer to God all that we would become,
our energy, our imagination,
to prepare our hearts to meet him.
Prepare the way of the Lord.
Make his paths straight.

God of constancy and change,
help us to recognize where we have become stuck
in the ruts of our familiar lives.
Break through our tired repetitions and jaded responses.
Prepare your way in us, make our paths straight,
that we might welcome your Son,
Jesus, the child who is to come.
Amen.

Blessing

God in our hoping,
strength in our waiting,
love in our fearing,
peace in our preparing,
be now among us,
child who is coming,
bring us your blessing,
now and always.
Amen.

Hymn

Candlemas

Presentation of Christ in the Temple

A sample service sheet for the service on page 185.

COMFORT AND CHALLENGE
IN OUR DARKNESS

Gathering Chant

> The kingdom of God is justice and peace
> and joy in the Holy Spirit.
> Come, Lord, and open in us
> the gates of your kingdom. (Taizé)

Opening Prayer

Child of our longing,
hope of ancient days,
comfort for the lowly,
challenge for the proud,
you come to challenge our established structures of power,
you come for the falling and rising of many.
Come now and open our hearts
to your presence in our midst.
Amen.

Prayers of Preparation

Mary and Joseph brought the sacrifice of the poor,
a pair of turtle doves,
all they could afford,
to give thanks for the birth of their son.
Lord Jesus, what shall we bring?
(Silence)

We come with empty hands.
Fill us with your grace.

Simeon and Anna waited patiently in the Temple,
hoping and longing
for God's promises to be fulfilled.
Lord Jesus, what shall we hope for?
(Silence)

We come with empty hands.
Fill us with your grace.

We come to this place, to this moment,
offering all that we are,
all that we have,
all that we hope to become.
Lord Jesus, we come to you.
(Silence)

We come with empty hands.
Fill us with your grace.

Prayers of Confession

The Lord whom you seek
will suddenly come to his temple.
The messenger of the covenant in whom you delight,
indeed, he is coming, says the Lord of hosts.
But who can endure the day of his coming,

and who can stand when he appears?
For he is like a refiner's fire and like fullers' soap;
he will sit as a refiner and purifier of silver.
(Malachi 3.1–3)

We hold a time of silence as we remember how much God loves us

Chant

Kyrie, kyrie, kyrie eleison (Taizé)
(We sing the chant after each prayer)

Loving God, refining fire,
you know us through and through;
nothing is hidden from your gaze.
You look for the best in us,
you look beyond our faults and failings,
you look into our hearts.
Lord, have mercy on us,
Kyrie, Kyrie, Kyrie eleison.

Loving God, refining fire,
we hardly know ourselves,
we hide behind false images;
we can too easily look for
the worst in ourselves and in others,
failing to look below the surface.
(Silence)

Lord, have mercy on us,
Kyrie, kyrie, kyrie eleison.

Loving God, refining fire,
help us to see through your eyes,
like Simeon and Anna,
to see the opportunities you present,
the promises you fulfil,

to see the best in ourselves and in others,
and to live from that perception.
(Silence)

Lord, have mercy on us,
Kyrie, kyrie, kyrie eleison.

The Assurance of Forgiveness

God for us
in our becoming,
God with us
in our journeying,
God in us
in our healing.
God, Father, Son and Holy Spirit,
forgive us and make us whole.
Amen.

Responsive Psalm – *Psalm 67*

**Let the peoples praise you, O God;
let all the peoples praise you.**

May God be gracious to us and bless us,
and make his face to shine upon us,
that your way may be known upon earth,
your saving power among all nations.
**Let the peoples praise you, O God;
let all the peoples praise you.**

Let the nations be glad and sing for joy,
for you judge the peoples with equity
and guide all the nations upon earth.
**Let the peoples praise you, O God;
let all the peoples praise you.**

The earth has yielded its increase;
God, our God, has blessed us.
May God continue to bless us;
let all the ends of the earth revere him.
Let the peoples praise you, O God;
let all the peoples praise you.

Chant

Jesus, your Spirit in us
is a wellspring of life everlasting (Taizé)

Reading – *Luke 2.22–24*

When the time came for their purification according to the law
of Moses, Mary and Joseph brought Jesus up to Jerusalem to
present him to the Lord (as it is written in the law of the Lord,
'Every firstborn male shall be designated as holy to the Lord'),
and they offered a sacrifice according to what is stated in the law
of the Lord, 'a pair of turtle-doves or two young pigeons.'

Reflection

Silence
How can I live sacrificially?

Chant

Jesus, your Spirit in us
is a wellspring of life everlasting (Taizé)

Reading – *Luke 2.25–28*

Now there was a man in Jerusalem whose name was Simeon;
this man was righteous and devout, looking forward to the consolation of Israel, and the Holy Spirit rested on him. It had been
revealed to him by the Holy Spirit that he would not see death
before he had seen the Lord's Messiah. Guided by the Spirit,

Simeon came into the temple; and when the parents brought in the child Jesus, to do for him what was customary under the law, Simeon took him in his arms and praised God, saying,

Now, Lord, you let your servant go in peace:
your word has been fulfilled.
My own eyes have seen the salvation
which you have prepared in the sight of every people;
A light to reveal you to the nations
and the glory of your people Israel.
(*Common Worship*)

Reading - *Luke 2.33-35*

And the child's father and mother were amazed at what was being said about him. Then Simeon blessed them and said to his mother Mary, 'This child is destined for the falling and the rising of many in Israel, and to be a sign that will be opposed so that the inner thoughts of many will be revealed – and a sword will pierce your own soul too.'

Reflection

Silence
In our own lives, what needs changing?

Chant

Jesus, your Spirit in us
is a wellspring of life everlasting (Taizé)

Reading - *Luke 2.36-40*

There was also a prophet, Anna the daughter of Phanuel, of the tribe of Asher. She was of a great age, having lived with her husband seven years after her marriage, then as a widow to the age of 84. She never left the temple but worshipped there with fasting and prayer night and day. At that moment she came, and began to praise God and to speak about the child to all who were looking for the redemption of Jerusalem.

When they had finished everything required by the law of the Lord, they returned to Galilee, to their own town of Nazareth. The child grew and became strong, filled with wisdom; and the favour of God was upon him.

Reflection

Silence
What is it that God has in store for you?
What is your core purpose?

Prayers of Intercession

Chant

Nothing can trouble,
Nothing can frighten.
Those who seek God
shall never go wanting.
Nothing can trouble,
Nothing can frighten.
God alone fills us. (Taizé)
(We sing the chant after each prayer)

Child of the poor,
hope of the outcast,
delight of the unloved,
you come to us in helpless vulnerability.
Be with all those who feel helpless and vulnerable now.
Nothing can trouble ...

Child in the temple,
greeted by Simeon,
light of the nations,
you come to bring light to dark places.

Be with all who struggle in darkness now.
Nothing can trouble ...

Child of the people,
recognized by Anna,
bringing us freedom,
you come to those who long for freedom.
Be with all who are held in bondage now.
Nothing can trouble ...

Child of justice,
destined for the falling and rising of many,
you come to turn us upside down.
Be with all who long for justice now.
Nothing can trouble ...

Child of perception,
you come to reveal our inner thoughts,
to call us to yourself.
Be with all who have lost their way now.
Nothing can trouble ...

Child of opposition,
you come to call us to a different way,
to challenge the values of our world.
Be with us as we walk your way of transforming love.
Nothing can trouble ...

Our Father, who art in heaven,
hallowed be thy name;
thy kingdom come,
thy will be done,
on earth as it is in heaven.
Give us this day our daily bread.
And forgive us our trespasses,
as we forgive those who trespass against us.
And lead us not into temptation,
but deliver us from evil.

For thine is the kingdom, the power, and the glory,
for ever and ever.
Amen.

Candle Lighting

*Music is played as we come forward to light candles around
the cross to renew our commitment to shine as lights in the
darkness, and to ask God to shine through our living*

Blessing

Bless to us your light in our darkness;
bless to us your hope in our hearts;
bless to us your peace in our homes.
And the blessing of God,
Father, Son and Holy Spirit,
be with us,
now and for ever.
Amen.

Final Chant

In the Lord I'll be ever thankful
In the Lord I will rejoice!
Trust in God, do not be afraid.
Lift up your voices, the Lord is near.
Lift up your voices, the Lord is near. (Taizé)

Resources

Music for Reflection – *also available from other sites*

A Gaelic Blessing – John Rutter
www.amazon.co.uk/s/ref=nb_sb_noss?url=search-alias%3Ddigital-
music&field-keywords=Rutter+gaelic+blessing

Lalalala Gohle Laleh, from Lullabies from the Axis of Evil
https://itunes.apple.com/gb/album/lullabies-from-axis-evil/id928110672

Le Onde – Ludovico Einaudi
www.amazon.co.uk/s/ref=nb_sb_noss?url=search-alias%3Ddigital-
music&field-keywords=les+onde+einaudi

Mass for four voices: Agnus Dei – William Byrd
www.amazon.co.uk/d/gh3/Mass-for-four-voices-VI-Agnus-dei/
Boo2SS1E5W

Nunc Dimittis – Arvo Pärt
www.amazon.co.uk/Estonian-Philharmonic-Chamber-Choir-Hillier/dp/
B00B4K8QKG

O nobilissima viriditas – Hildegard of Bingen
www.allmusic.com/album/hildegard-von-bingen-o-nobilissima-
viriditas-mw0001407406

O viriditas digiti Dei – Hildegard of Bingen
www.amazon.com/O-viriditas-digiti-dei/dp/B0013AIWBA

O viridissima Virga ave – Hildegard of Bingen
www.allmusic.com/song/vision-the-music-of-hildegard-von-bingeno-
viridissima-virga-ave-mt0004554885

Pavan – William Byrd
www.amazon.co.uk/Pavane-William-Byrd/dp/B016FOQGHK

Peter Grimes: Act 1, The Storm – Benjamin Britten
www.amazon.co.uk/s/ref=nb_sb_noss?url=search-alias%3Ddigital-music&field-keywords=Benjamin+britten+peter+grimes+the+storm

Song for Athene – John Tavener
www.amazon.co.uk/s/ref=nb_sb_noss?url=search-alias%3Ddigital-music&field-keywords=Tavener+song+for+athene

Spiegel im Spiegel – Arvo Pärt
www.amazon.co.uk/Arvo-Part-Spiegel-im/dp/B0036ULAKK

The Armed Man: Benedictus – Karl Jenkins
www.amazon.co.uk/s/ref=nb_sb_ss_i_9_12?url=search-alias%3Ddigital-music&field-keywords=karl+jenkins+benedictus&sprefix=Karl+jenkins%2Cdigital-music%2C144&crid=1HQZ3Y3CZV28S

Whirling Winds – Ludovico Einaudi
www.amazon.co.uk/s/ref=nb_sb_noss?url=search-alias%3Ddigital-music&field-keywords=einaudi+whirling+winds

Hymns, songs and chants

Most of the Christmas carols are traditional and well known and not included in this list.

A new commandment	(tune: New Commandment)
Abba Father	Dave Bilbrough
All hail the power of Jesus' name	Edward Perronet (tune: Coronation (Holden))
Amazing Grace	John Newton
Be still, for the presence of the Lord	David Evans, Thank You Music
Be thou my vision	Words by Mary E. Byrne and Eleanor H. Hull (tune: Slane)
Behold, I make all things new	John L. Bell, Wild Goose Worship
Bless the Lord, my soul	Taizé Community
Blessed be your name	Matt Redman
Break our hearts	Vicky Beeching
Brightest and best of the sons of the morning	Reginald Heber

Christ's is the world in which we move	John L. Bell (tune: Dream Angus)
Cloth for the cradle	John L. Bell (tune: Wae's for me, Prince Charlie)
Come down, O Love divine	Bianco da Siena (tune: Down Ampney)
Come, thou long expected Jesus	Charles Wesley
Confitemini Domino	Taizé Community
Days of Elijah	Robin Mark
Dear Lord and Father	John Greenleaf Whittier (1872) (tune: Rest)
Do not be afraid	Gerard Markland
Don't be afraid	John L. Bell (Wild Goose Worship)
Empty, broken, here I stand	Nick Haigh, Anita Haigh, Northumbria Community
Father, hear the prayer we offer	Love M. Whitcomb Willis
Father, I place into your hands	Jenny Hewer
Fill your hearts with joy and gladness	Timothy Dudley-Smith (tune: Ode to Joy)
For the healing of the nations	Fred Kaan (1965)
Give thanks with grateful heart	Henry Smith (tune: Give Thanks (Smith))
Glory and gratitude and praise	John L. Bell, Wild Goose Worship
Go forth and tell	J. E. Seddon
God's spirit is in my heart	Alan Dale and Hubert J. Richards (tune: Go tell everyone)
Goodness is stronger than evil	Desmond Tutu, music by John L. Bell
Great is the darkness	Gerald Coates and Noël Richards
Guide me, O Thou great Redeemer	William Williams, translated by Peter Williams
Heaven shall not wait	Graham Maule and John L. Bell
Here in this place	Marty Haugen (tune: Gather us in)
Here we will welcome	Andrew Pratt (tune: Stewardship)

I heard the voice of Jesus say	Horatius Bonar
I will change your name	D. J. Butler, Vineyard Music
I will offer up my life	Matt Redman
I, the Lord of sea and sky	Daniel L. Schutte (1981) (tune: Here I am, Lord)
In Christ alone	Stuart Townend
In our darkness	Taizé Community
In the Lord I'll be ever thankful	Taizé Community
Inspired by love and anger	John L. Bell and Graham Maule (tune: Salley Gardens)
Jesus Christ the apple tree	From Divine Hymns or Spiritual Songs, Joshua Smith
Jesus, be the centre	Michael Frye, Vineyard Music
Jesus, your Spirit in us	Taizé Community
Kyrie	Taizé Community
Kyrie, Kyrie, Kyrie eleison	Taizé Community
Laudate omnes gentes	Taizé Community
Light of the world	Chris Tomlin, 'Here I am to worship'
Lo, he comes with clouds descending	Charles Wesley (1758)
Longing for light	Bernadette Farrell (tune: Christ, be our light)
Lord, for the years	Timothy Dudley Smith
Magnificat	Taizé Community
Make me a channel of your peace	St Francis of Assisi, adapted by Sebastian Temple
Make way! Make way!	Graham Kendrick
Mayenziwe	John L. Bell, Wild Goose Worship
Men of faith, rise up and sing	Martin Smith, Curious? Music
Nothing can trouble	Taizé Community
O breath of life	Bessie Porter Head
O Christmas tree	Translated by H. Brueckner (1926) (tune: Maryland)

O God of earth and altar	G. K. Chesterton
O God, our help in ages past	Isaac Watts (tune: St Anne)
O Lord, hear my prayer	Taizé Community
O Thou who camest from above	Charles Wesley
O worship the Lord	John Samuel Bewley Monsell
On Jordan's bank	Charles Coffin (tune: Winchester New)
Purify my heart	Brian Doerksen (tune: Refiner's Fire)
Restore, O Lord, the honour	Graham Kendrick and Chris Rolinson
Rock of ages	Augustus Toplady
Sing hey for the carpenter	John L. Bell and Graham Maule (tune: Sing hey)
Sing of the Lord's goodness	Ernest Sands (tune: Sing of the Lord's Goodness)
Sing to God	Michael Baughen (tune: Hymn to Joy)
Stand, O stand firm	John L. Bell, Wild Goose Worship
Take, O take me	John L. Bell, Wild Goose Worship
Teach me to dance	Graham Kendrick
Tell out, my soul	Timothy Dudley Smith
The cedar of Lebanon	Richard Littledale (tune: Cedar)
The kingdom of God is justice and peace	Taizé Community
The Lord is my light	Taizé Community
The Lord's my shepherd	Stuart Townend
The splendour of the King	Chris Tomlin, Hillsong Music
Through all the changing scenes of life	Nahum Tate and Nicholas Brady (tune: Wiltshire)
Thy hand, O God, has guided	E. H. Plumptre (tune: Thornbury)
Touch the earth lightly	Shirley Erena Murray (tune: Tenderness – Gibson)
Ubi Caritas	Taizé Community

List of Illustrations

The publisher and author acknowledge with thanks permission to use photographs and illustrations under copyright. Every effort has been made to contact the sources and we would be grateful to be informed of any omissions. Wikimedia Commons images are used by a Creative Commons Attribution-ShareAlike 3.0 licence.

Page